P9-DMC-019

19995

POETIC VALUES:

THEIR REALITY AND OUR NEED OF THEM

POETIC VALUES

*Their Reality and Our
Need of Them*

BY

JOHN G. NEIHARDT

25659

𝔑𝔢𝔴 𝔜𝔬𝔯𝔨

THE MACMILLAN COMPANY

1925

All rights reserved

YORK COLLEGE
Library No. 19995

Copyright, 1925.
By THE MACMILLAN COMPANY.

———

Set up and electrotyped.
Published November, 1925.

PRINTED IN THE UNITED STATES OF AMERICA BY
THE CORNWALL PRESS

BH
39
.N4

70~~1~~.~~17~~

~~N397~~

NOTE

In the following lectures, prepared for a university audience, I have undertaken to suggest for the common-sense man, who sometimes doubts the wisdom of the prevailing view of life, a means by which he might come to think of poetic values as real, and necessarily integral in the scale of practical values. It will be seen that by the term "poetic values" I refer to something more important than a literary form.

I should feel less hopeful about my purpose if my claim to originality were greater. Most of the things I have to say have been said in one form or another; but, so far as I know, they have not been said together and related for the present purpose. The view I take of human consciousness is as old as the older *Upanishads* and as new as modern psychology; and were it merely old I would not have taken it. It is the empirical nature of the new and its correspondence with the old, within the range of our experience, that seems to indicate the possibility of a practical synthetic view of our values. My debt to F. W. H. Myers is the debt of modern psychology; and it would be well if my readers were familiar with the third chapter of *Human Personality*. In the 80's, Charles Howard Hinton, in a series of works, notably *A New Era of Thought,* undertook some such synthesis of values as is here suggested; but his argument was based upon the conception of higher space and multiple dimensionality, an interesting but vague conjecture likely to convince no one. Recently, P. D. Ouspensky, in *Tertium Organum,* greatly elaborated Hinton's theory, his purpose being that of the idealistic monist. He undertakes to demolish science, and restates, in substance, the Oriental conception of the universe as consciousness. In the course of his argument he accounts ingeniously for the genesis of higher values; but one wonders why he should be concerned with values at all, since he reasons toward a negation of all that we can know of the world. The conscious states that he employs, by way of proceeding from the illusion of finite dimensionality to the universal negation of the infinite, are not those of experimental psychology, but are mere abstractions, unrelated to our experience. They are merely phases of decreasing illusion in Universal Consciousness, of which my reader and I know nothing.   Such speculations as those of Hinton and Ouspensky are valuable in that they tend to engender healthy doubts as to the necessary validity of our customary thought-patterns; and both have suggested thought-patterns to me, which I have employed, however, to an end differing from theirs as experimental psychology differs from metaphysics.

Perhaps most practical men would regard any discussion of reality as a waste of time.   But our conception of values, by which we live, must grow out of our genuine belief as to what is real.   As to the conception of reality employed in the following pages, it will be seen to be based upon a higher Vedanist view, though I have undertaken to state it in terms of our psychology.   Ananda Coomaraswamy, in his chapter on the Vedanta in *Buddha and the Gospel of Buddhism,* states it thus: "Seen from the standpoint of our empirical consciousness, it is veritably the real that is reflected through the doorways of our senses, and takes the forms of our imagination.   Here the phenomenal world is not without significance, but has just so much significance as the degree of our enlightenment allows us to discover in it. . . . *Our partial view is false in so far, and only in so far, as it is partial.*"

NOTE

Among American philosophers I have been influenced especially by John Elof Boodin, whose *Realistic Universe* presents a profound study of the whole problem of which the question here considered is an implied minor phase. The degree in which I should wish to acknowledge Dr. Boodin's influence is limited only by my fear of misrepresenting the scope, the beauty and even, in some ways, the direction of his thought.

In *The Manhood of Humanity*, Count Korzybski approached the matter with which we are concerned through the conception of space values and time values, as distinguishing brute from man. He was not concerned with the mechanism by which such values are realized. The profound significance of his idea, as applied to social problems, seems not to have gotten far—perhaps for the very reasons that prompted him to write his book.

The question, how shall we be human? has been discussed from many angles, for is it not the greatest question in the world? Perhaps it may yet be shown that all answers are the same in meaning, however disguised by various terminologies and rituals. But before such a simplified answer could be generally understood, the need of an answer would have ceased.

NOTE

Our concern here is with the human necessity of taking into account a great deal more of the world than is generally considered. We assume that every man is conscious of a portion or phase of the world. It may be that our world is illusion to angelic intelligence; but, even so, it is, in the main, a constant illusion for us. Its constancies must be our realities, and the name doesn't matter. Call it illusion; but since we are as we are, we shall have to learn how to live in all of it, whatever it is.

We have nothing to do with the infinite, the absolute, but try to keep to what we can agree to regard as known. Perhaps we have facts enough to save us—a sufficient quantity of broken glass to make some sort of window pane through which to view our immediate world, if we can only agree to fuse some of the fragments.

JOHN G. NEIHARDT.

I

COMMON SENSE

I

COMMON SENSE

I suppose everyone has heard more times than he can recollect that saying with which some cynical quip on human nature—the other man's human nature—is very often greeted. Let someone express a flippant half-truth on, let us say, the very doubtful merits of a prospering neighbor, or on the hopeless illogicality of womankind in general, or on the probable hypocrisy of one who consents to be accounted pious, or on the hypothetical nature of matrimonial felicity, and very likely some hearer with a phonographic mind will feel himself under compulsion to remark: "Well, there's more truth than poetry in that!" Whereupon all present chuckle once again over a remark so original and illuminating.

As a first aid for cases of intellectual collapse, this saying seems to be employed in practically every stratum of society. I assume its almost universal use because I myself have often heard it used in the lower as well as in some of the higher and more frosty social and intellectual latitudes. I have heard it from the lowly farmer, vocally groping after a solution for the twin mystery of price and politics; and I have heard it from the lips of inspired shoe-salesmen, holding forth with burly assurance in the blue, Olympian air of smoking cars. I can go no farther upward, that being, so far as I know, the dizzy limit, too dangerously near the lightnings of the Lord; for in my years of compulsory travel about the country I have come to regard the drummer as second only to the hotel clerk in wisdom.

Now there may be a sense in which it is true, as we have been taught, that the voice of the People is the voice of God, though there are those gloomy philosophers who profess to have detected a distinct braying note in the music of the Many. Being neither gloomy nor a philosopher, I prefer to believe that popular utterances do indeed convey truth in an enigmatic form; and is it not well within the range of practical theology to assume that truth partakes of the nature of Divinity? I suppose there is, as yet, no certain method for riddling the Delphic utterances of the multitude; but in a great many instances, at least, this can be done by the simple process of reversal. That is to say, if nearly everybody seems to be saying it, it is probably wrong; for quantity and quality are, as yet, only theoretically synonymous, however "un-American" the remark may be.

"More truth than poetry!" It is because I believe that popular utterances are likely to be pregnant with meaning that I purpose to examine this particular stop-gap for intellectual vacuity by way of approach to my theme; for I suspect that it reveals some misapprehension of what may prove to be the deepest things in human life.

It must be granted that the person who uses this expression probably has no very definite thought in mind. He is simply repeating by rote certain sounds that stand for an attitude so deep-seated that he never examines it, and it is such deep-seated convictions that determine the trends of the world.

Knowing, as we do, the complexion of the general mind, whose processes are untroubled by definition, what may we safely assume to be the nature of this truth which seems, by implication, to be not only opposed to poetry, but vastly superior to it? The answer is obvious. Truth, in the meaning of our catch phrase, is simply common sense in its most

YORK COLLEGE LIBRARY

dogmatic form. It is the sort of truth popularly described as "getting down to brass tacks." The extreme devotees of such truth are likely to be loud in the praise of their own practicality. You cannot fool them, for they know their world. It is snugly limited, except possibly on Sunday, by the five senses naïvely regarded as infallible. Seeing, to them, is believing. Hard cash is the measure of value; and the question, "What am I getting out of it?" is the sole criterion of justifiable effort. I am sure that many who profess such an attitude in public are at times more than a trifle doubtful of it in private; for there is no fixed level of intelligence, and always the pressure of mystery about us is immense. But it is a significant fact that most conversations one overhears in public places, where men feel themselves under compulsion to seem worldly wise, is dominated by this conception; and woe to the luckless enthusiast who ventures to oppose it!

We might venture much farther in our description of this prevalent attitude, with no great fear of erring. We might even show how, as a result of it, money-getting has taken on the characteristics of fanatical religious passion; and this is not strange, for what is religion, at bottom, but one's attitude toward that in which one most profoundly

believes?[1] And who that is observing has not
sensed the attitude of holiness surrounding great
wealth; noted the exaggerated deference with which
the most commonplace representative of great
wealth is received, even in circles otherwise distinguished by intelligence? Once as an editorial writer
I ventured upon an oblique remark calculated to
throw some slight shadow of doubt upon the inevitable righteousness of Big Business, and, being
called upon the carpet, I was informed in bellowing
tones that "Business is sacred!" The statement
was no mere expression of individual opinion; it was
an authentic echo from our loud world. I once had
the honor of being invited to a banquet given by an
organization of advertising men. It was a "pep"
meeting, and a celebrated "pep" speaker had been
employed to dispense the Gospel. Gospel is the correct word. It was truly an evangelistic performance,
and one had only to make a few justifiable substi-
tutions in the speaker's terminology to fancy himself
as being inadvertently present at a good old revival
meeting of the classic vulgar type. Verily it seemed
that souls were to be snatched into a state of ecstatic

[1] "Religion is the serious and social attitude of individuals or
communities toward the power or powers which they conceive
as having ultimate control over their interests and destinies."—
Pratt: *The Religious Consciousness*.

efficiency for the greater glory of some barbaric god. The response of the audience was deafening; nor was I a scoffer in that temple; for, potentially, the religious sense is precious beyond computation, however unworthy, at the moment, may be the object of its worship; and so long as it is strong in men, there is good reason to hope that some new world-psychosis may serve to employ it in the furthering of values more worthy of human regard. As I have said, I do not believe that this state of mind is absolute in even the least intelligent of human beings, for we live in mystery and some glimmering of awe must at times break through upon the darkest mind. Nevertheless it is true that this attitude is the insubstantial despot of our time that all but a relative few obey, and those who do not obey are punished.

Now what, in the extreme meaning of our catch phrase, may poetry be? Simply "hokum" set to rhyme; a thing to which one may descend in occasional sentimental moods, but always with one's fingers figuratively crossed, and with the distinct understanding that of course one knows better and that it is "no fair" to tag an otherwise practical man caught in the act. For, after all, home *is* sweet and mother *is* dear and the little birdies *do* sometimes twitter sweetly in the morning. One must have relaxation; one cannot always be brooding on those brain-taxing profundities, the contemplation of which doubtless explains much of the pontifical bearing of a certain successful business type. A very good brand of such poetical notions, we understand, is now being put out by Guest, Braley & Co., easily the leading manufacturers in this particular line of goods. Strictly modern factories, operated on strictly up-to-date business principles, quantity production, standardization of parts, reduction of overhead to a minimum—if not quite to the vanishing point—have resulted in a price that places the commodity within easy reach of all. No previous experience demanded of the consumer.

But since it is apparent that our practical gentleman is somewhat embarrassed by our discovery of his momentary weakness, let us withdraw that he may the more readily regain his dignity, meanwhile giving our attention to more serious matters. Later, if we can feel assured that no practical person is present, we shall return to the subject of poetry, for it seems that something may have been overlooked. At present we shall limit our attention to the first half of our catch phrase by way of determining, if we can, the nature and implications of that

truth which is contrasted with poetry, apparently
little to the credit of the latter.

To the general consciousness of the multitude in
which this despotic mood of sordid utilitarianism
exists, it is as though the prevailing scale of values
had always prevailed; as though mankind had
always been concerned chiefly with the accumulation
of that which represents the power to gratify the
physical needs and many clamoring lusts of animal
life. Since the general consciousness is given over
almost wholly to those values which may be described only in spatial terms, it is not strange that
the moment in which we seem to live, that moment
which is no more than an imaginary link between
memory and desire, should take on the illusion of
a spatial permanence. But as many individuals,
who go to make up the multitude, are themselves
aware, the prevailing psychosis as to the supreme
importance of material things is of recent origin.
A little over a century ago the social center of
gravity was apparently as firmly fixed in the conception of a spiritual world as now in what may prove
to be quite as questionable a conception of a material world; for it is characteristic of the multitude
to grasp at a guess in the dark and to worship its
latest guess, until some exterior stimulus breaks

through to muddle the old dream and to furnish a key suggestion about which a new dream may take form. I do not insist that this likening of mass consciousness to that of an individual dreamer should be taken figuratively; for the cases are similar; and alas for the searcher after truth who shall fall asleep in the Many!

The central fact in the complexity of circumstances that served to shift the social center of gravity was economic. Mechanical invention, resulting in the Industrial Revolution in England; the rise of Capitalism; the emergence and triumph of the trading class in the French Revolution; the concurrent development of economic, philosophic and scientific theory in keeping with the growing mood, and the deepening of the mood by virtue of the theories that grew out of it—these, and other factors, interacting and aided by a steadily increasing pressure of need among the masses and of greed among the masters of machines, served to shift the focus of social attention. The shift was from the promised rewards and punishments of a world to be reached only by dying to a world in which one must live—a world whose punishments by freezing and starvation and human scorn might well make the climate of a remote and increasingly problematical hell seem quite Californian, and whose possible rewards outdazzled with a compelling immediacy the faint, far glimmer of the gates of pearl.

No doubt there are those who would insist at this point that no such wholesale shifting of attention has taken place, submitting as evidence the fact that thousands upon thousands still go to church and worship as of old. But is it not true that genuine belief is a subconscious attitude, revealed only by the main direction of striving; a matter of spontaneous, as distinguished from voluntary, attention; and that the individuals of which the mass is composed may consciously hold to that which unconsciously they repudiate? It is not to individual minds that one must go to determine the dominating belief of the time, but to the general consciousness revealed in the object of its spontaneous attention. And certainly no one would contend that the laying up of treasures in heaven beyond the reach of moth and rust and the income tax is to be regarded as even one of the key industries of the United States.

Fancy a citizen of another planet formulating a report for his people after a tour of investigation among us here. Consider that our celestial visitor could in no way be influenced in his judgments by those tangled vestiges of old thought and emotion wherewith we strive so valiantly to rationalize the costly conflict between our professions and our effective beliefs. What would he be likely to report as to the nature of the deity we worship? Might he not easily mistake our banking houses for temples, where daily in a hush of sanctity the priesthood functions in the awful Presence, dispensing to all comers, according to their deserts, the holy wafers that alone have power to save? And would he not be profoundly impressed by the fanatical intensity of yearning for such salvation displayed in the rough-and-tumble struggle of our world?

I know that there has long been a saying to the effect that Americans worship the dollar; and it may be that the first man who said it intended to make a literal statement of an observed fact. But the saying has passed so often through the bath of the multitude that its meaning has been washed away, and it has become, as so many tremendous statements of truth have become by the same process, no more than a harmless platitude—harmless, indeed, as the most explosive utterances of the Nazarene have become harmless—so harmless that even a hypocrite may juggle them freely, and they won't go off! The process is simple and quite democratically within reach of all. One has only to remember the words by way of appearing good and wise; and forget the implications by way of remaining safe. To repeat such a platitude with a passionate conviction engendered by a vivid sense of its original meaning is to make a contribution to the art of living; for a platitude is a statement of truth that, having originated in a broader field of attention, has lost its meaning by becoming current in a narrower.

However, I think many will grant that the religious sense, as now operating in the multitude, has exchanged a spiritual for a material scale of values; that it is still truly the religious sense, however it may be disguised or denied; and that the fact of the transference dominates our time.

That word truth, then, as used in our catch phrase, "more truth than poetry," may be tracked from its simplest connotation as dogmatic common sense to its sublimation by the inevitable religious sense into what may truly be called the practically universal awe of Money. I am sure we can say, without exaggeration, that, virtually, Money has been deified in our time by an unconscious process; and that the underlying reason for this is practically the same as that which led the ancient Egyptians

to find divinity in the cat. The terrible rats of
human need, and salvation therefrom, are at the bottom of this preposterous twentieth century superstition. And yet, why should not the multitude give
its genuine worship to a joss so mighty? A dozen
devotees may supplicate a dozen different deities,
all theoretically omnipotent, yet, lacking the saving
grace of Mammon, the children of each may grow
up like rodents in the midst of a world well dotted
with temples and mosques and churches and syna-
gogues—a world that, more than once, has been
died for by spiritual saviors. We know that this
is possible because it is right now happening to
millions in the centers of civilization. Is it any matter for wonder that an abject money-awe should be
all but universal in effect? And in whatever form
it may be found, it is sure to be concerned, no doubt
unconsciously, as a rule, with the same smug limitation of the world by the five senses.

Truly, where one's treasure is, there will his heart
be also; and where the heart is, there shall center
the activities of the religious sense, however one may
fail to recognize it for what it is. And whenever
this sense works in the mass, a dogma springs up
and grows and spreads, always rooting itself in the
dearest things men know, until it seems that any-

one who may venture to question it must be either dolt or villain. Any well-developed religious passion will not lack the sanction of authority, regarded as infallible, and accepted, in the last analysis, by a pure act of faith. That sanction of an infallible authority has, in our time, been furnished by physical science.

It is at this point that our popular catch phrase, "more truth than poetry," really begins to trouble us impractical people who believe in poetic values. So long as we were dealing with the attitude of the unlettered Philistine we could treat the saying with amusement; but we have followed common sense too far for laughter now, and we have come upon the all but absolute master of our world, the august pontiff of an unrecognized but, nevertheless, operative religion whereby most men, either consciously or unconsciously, conduct their lives. Perhaps we were a bit too bold in treating lightly the attitude of the shoe-salesman and the hotel clerk and the business evangelist with his up-and-at-'em gospel of pep, seeing that they have a friend so mighty; for what is Physical Science but Common Sense grown up and highly sophisticated? If we should urge our values upon the orthodox moneyac, might he not point out to us that our values are merely imaginary; that science has found no field of reality to which we may relate our so-called values; that money is the social means whereby the values of scientific reality may be controlled; and that one who mistakes imaginary values for real is simply in need of a guardian? Surely, we devotees of the poetic are in a sad position in this hustling world of established certainties. There was a time when we had authority to relate our values to the soul; but physical science has searched the cosmos very carefully, looking into many things and behind many things, from atoms to suns, and has found no trace of soul anywhere. Extremely impractical people suggest that perhaps the soul was itself concerned in the process of searching, as though one should go hunting for his glasses all about the house, never suspecting that they were, all the time, on his nose, else he could not have been searching at all. But no such fantastic notion is going to get far in this shrewd world—not in business hours. Such ideas are well enough for Sunday, the day when a practical man may cry "King's X" in the strenuous game of tag with Reality. So there is little hope for us just now in that direction.

It is true that capable makers in all the arts are allowed to live in this highly practical world, if they can. Often they can, if they are lucky. Some are even well endowed with genuine, that is to say, bankable values, in return for their efforts to entertain their fellow-men. Honors also are often generously bestowed. But these facts have not the meaning they may seem to have. More and more in our time it has become the proper thing to say that poetry, for instance, creates a world of imagination into which one may escape at times from the stress of reality. But if poetry (and by poetry we mean the essence of all the arts) has no greater function than that, then the practical person should employ not a poet, but a bootlegger. It is rumored that some of the more logical do. I have not the latest quotations on our rival's commodity; but considering that time is money, and that much time is required in preparing for a genuine appreciation of the poetic values, we may be sure that our competitor's offering is far cheaper; and I am told that as a *reality-killer* its virtues are unquestionably superior.

It is clear that we cannot afford to make any such compromise with the practical man, for upon such a basis we cannot hope to compete. Our overhead is too great. We must insist that it is not less reality that we want, but more; that our values are as real as any others, and that they must be regarded as actually integral in any sane scheme of human life, for reasons that will appear.

Thus we arouse an old antagonism, a quick sense of which must have been noted when one, who has been called a poet, first mentioned science as though there might possibly be something wrong with it; and who is a poet that he should think so? Philosophically, this antagonism is at least as old as Aristotle and Plato; psychically, as old as the dreaming of Man in a world of brutal actualities that somehow did not seem to run from even the bravest dream. So deeply is it rooted in human nature that it has divided our world geographically into temperamental hemispheres; and "East is East and West is West, and never the twain shall meet." It is as though there were literally two worlds, existing, as we might say, interpenetratively, yet of such widely different constitutions that no definite communication could be established between them, and each must regard the other as the illusion of a dream.

A number of years ago a Hindu Brahmin, on his way across the continent, spent a night and a day with me, giving as his justification for the loss of time (time, as we know, being money), that he was a very practical man and therefore never failed to call upon a poet when he could. We did not meet as strangers, for in my feverishly groping 'teens I had been far more powerfully moved by Vedantist conceptions than by any faith widely held in the Occident. Nevertheless we went to the mat at once and we wrestled into the small hours, to no fall, he taking the Oriental, subjective view of the world, and I the Occidental, objective view, as we like to think of it. He was telling me, in effect, that my view of the world was an illusion, and he proved it by pointing out what a mess we Occidentals have made of life. I was telling him that his world was wholly imaginary, and I proved it by pointing out how little progress Orientals had made. Thereupon he attacked my notion of progress; and that was a very weak point that needed a vast amount of strenuous rationalizing on my part. If he had only condescended to apply that headlock which we call logic, I think he could have pinned me to the mat right there; but he stuck to intuition while I stuck to logic, and so there wasn't any fall. Many times it seemed to me that I had his shoulders nearly down; but he always eluded my hold as by magic, and was off again into the dizzy empyrean, and I could but wait until he consented to come down. It was magnificent, but it didn't seem to be argument.

Now it may be that my Brahmin friend was right; but, if so, his truth is of a quality far beyond the uses of men such as my reader and I, unless it is greatly modified with a generous infusion of what we regard as the brutal facts of our existence as men; but my friend would admit no such infusion. On the other hand, I am convinced that I was wrong; for, by implication, I was simply defending the meaning of our catch phrase, "more truth than poetry." In fact I was uneasily aware of doing just that; but, being an Occidental, I identified the Occidental conception with myself, and mine was no more than a patriotic defense. Most conceptions of truth are probably held in that way. People will fight for their truth because it is theirs. It is a personal matter, as a rule. And this accounts, no doubt, for the appalling ferocity of the inquisitorial mood, such as we experienced, for instance, when we were engaged in saving the world for liberty. Somehow truth involves the loss of self, as my Hindu friend would insist.

I think I can see now that it would have been just as well if my friend and I had gone to bed at a reasonable hour; for all the while we were strug-

YORK COLLEGE LIBRARY

gling, the livable truth was quietly escaping by a direction perpendicular to the axis of hostilities.

Now our desire is to approximate by reasonable means, if we can, that direction by which the livable truth escaped my Brahmin friend and me. In that direction, if at all, will be found a field of reality to which our poetic values may be related; and it must be such as a common-sense man might be led by his own methods to accept as real in a livable sense; for our world is one of many needs and greeds, and we are not going to cease to be scientific, since only by the scientific method can our needs and greeds be satisfied. There are those optimists who seem to hope that by a process of evolution (which is a magical word) our planet may ultimately be populated with men of cosmic consciousness, all aglow with love. But they admit that the time for such a consummation is remote, and in the meanwhile our poetic values must qualify for existence and respect in a crude empirical world. If it cannot be shown that they are real values in the world of struggling men, then they may be values for archangels, but not for us.

In seeking what we have called the perpendicular to the axis of hostilities, we may best begin at the opposite end of the axis from us; for, as a society, we are only too well convinced of the common-sense scientific view, and it is in need of no defense. At one end of this axis—the objective end—is the so-called truth of our catch phrase, a truth that, even in its most exalted form, is still concerned only with sensible factuality. At the other, the subjective end, is to be found what the sordid practical man would class as mere poetry, the stuff of dreams. It is the latter position that my Brahmin friend defended, and we may state his view briefly and simply; realizing, however, that no such statement could possibly do more than point the general direction of Oriental thought, a sublime structure, developed by countless sages through leisurely millenniums of silence. Also, we shall touch upon only one of the purer forms of the *Vedanta,* untainted with the superstitions of the rabble. It is these two extreme attitudes that our purpose demands—the extreme materialistic and idealistic attitudes of our catch phrase—for between them stretches the whole human range of deed and vision. Neither end alone is humanly livable. Somewhere along the axis there must be a region where a practicable synthetic realism is possible—a realism greatly extended beyond the values of the brute for which our world now strives hysterically.

Now in the matter of the fruitless discussion between my Brahmin friend and me, the fundamental difference in method was this: that while I strove to ground my little ladder of speculation upon what I deemed the solid facts of this everyday world of ours, thence reasoning outward into the unknown, and certainly not getting very far, he began with an absolute, thence working inward to this pathetic isolation that we Occidentals term reality, which, at best, to him, was a sort of intricately organized misunderstanding, and therefore a very bad place to begin. In my view, the Oriental knew everything and could prove nothing whatever. In his view, the Occidental knew nothing and would prove everything, pitifully convinced that anything knowable must be classifiable as information. The absolute with which he began was Bráhman, to be conceived as universal consciousness in which no conception of individuality could possibly exist. Bráhman was not represented as a god, not as *a* universal being, but rather as Universal Being. Individual consciousness, the ego in our terminology, he termed atman; and this atman, this self, was lost in an illusory world—Maya—illusion being the transient stuff of all human woe. The illusion, in another view of the doctrine, consists, not in the non-existence of the phenomenal world, but in the conception of individuality through which it can but be falsely conceived. The illusion lies in the partial view of the world, inevitable in the erroneous conception of individuality. But to him the truth was that there is only Bráhman, and to Bráhman the atman, or self, was as a drop of water to an infinite ocean; a drop of water conceiving itself apart from universal water. Only by attaining to the knowledge of oneness with the Sea could salvation from the woe that is of Maya —illusion—be achieved; only by the loss of self in the whole could Nirvana be attained; and Nirvana was not to be regarded as non-existence, but rather as universal existence. Proceeding, our Brahmin would point out the various stages or "stations" by which the illuded self may attain to deliverance in Nirvana; and the number of them, as set forth in the older *Upanishads,* is three: [1]

First: The Waking Consciousness, that in which men vividly conceive themselves as individuals and are exclusively aware of everyday experiences. This is the consciousness of scientific materialism; and it is a curious, and should be a disturbing, fact that

[1] Coomaraswamy, *Buddha and the Gospel of Buddhism.* Chap. on the Vedanta.

our civilization is virtually, though not avowedly, founded on the belief that this is the only valid state. "When the soul is blinded by glamour (Maya)," so reads one of the *Upanishads*, "it inhabits the body and accomplishes actions. By food, drink and many enjoyments it obtains satisfaction in a waking state."

Second: The State of Dream-Sleep. Says the *Upanishad:* "In the dream-state it (the individual self) moves up and down, and fashions for itself as gods many forms."

Third: The State of Deep Sleep. Therein the illusory sense of individuality is lost, with all its suffering, merging in Bráhman. "This," says the *Upanishad*, "is the true form of being, wherein it is raised above longing, free from evil and from fear. . . . Then the father is not the father, nor the mother mother, nor the worlds worlds." In that state, neither subject nor object is known, for subject and object have become one.

In the later *Upanishads* a fourth and more profound state is given; but we cannot consider it, since there is nothing in our experience to which it corresponds.

Offer this idealistic doctrine to a typical matter-of-fact money-worshipper for consideration, and he will demolish it with the simple ease of laughter; for he knows well what things are real, just as a horse or cow knows. But when one inquires into the original significance of the word Bráhman, one may reasonably begin to wonder if, after all, the count-less seers of India, meditating for unknown cen-turies in the silence of their forests, may not have anticipated a truth toward which we of the West have been laboring clumsily by means inadequate, and are only now beginning to realize. Max Müller tells us that the word Bráhman "seems to have meant originally *what bursts forth or breaks forth, whether in the shape of thought and word or in the shape of creative power or physical force*." [1]

It is at this point that we begin to feel hopeful of finding that direction perpendicular to the axis of apparent antagonism by which the livable truth is wont to escape us; and certainly it does escape; the direction in which a greatly extended objectivity may be sought—a synthetic realism, comprehending in an unbroken scale both the values that are essen-tial to animal existence and the values without which there can be no humanity, and no genuine civilization.

Now I cannot but sympathize heartily with the

[1] Müller: *The Vedanta Philosophy.* Lecture 1.

strictly common-sense man in his attitude toward any metaphysical conception of the universe, since I have found it no easy matter, at times, to procure the necessities of animal existence; and I certainly believe in the reality of such existence. But while I accept it as real, I agree with my Brahmin friend in this, that to regard it as the whole is truly to live in illusion, to be lost in Maya, as he would say. I cannot go the whole way with my practical friend, being convinced, as a result of forty-odd years of it, that animal existence in itself is dear at the price of a single twinge of tooth-ache, not to mention greater woes. On the other hand, I cannot go the whole way with my Brahmin friend. We of the West cannot go so far from that dear prejudice which is our home, even though free philosophical transportation be furnished. It may be that the universe is, somehow, consciousness and nothing else, but my reader and I cannot live as though it were. Truth, for us, must be limited to the livable. It is not yet, for us at least, a matter of absolute truth, if indeed there be such; but of our finite understanding. We shall have to make out with a conception of relative truth whereby we can live; but this must be the broadest humanly realizable truth; and that is what the common-sense man certainly has not, even by his own standards of judgment, as may appear.

As we proceed, we hope to find that the metaphysical conception of our Brahmin friend may correspond exactly, so far as our experience goes, with a certain modern Occidental conception based upon experiment; and that the latter may be substituted for the former, without doing violence to either, to the end that the bald and needed fact of the sordid common-sense attitude, together with the subtler, humanizing view of the opposite attitude, may be saved and related; that we may neither fall into the abyss of mere animality at one end of the axis, nor be called upon to qualify for existence in an abstract universe of pure consciousness at the other extreme.

We cannot begin with an absolute, or any infinite conception; there is nothing in our experience to correspond to infinity. The very conception cannot be other than a zero quantity in the speculations of men like my reader and me, whatever it might be to a highly developed Oriental seer. We are not threatened with any sudden access of infinite understanding. On the contrary, we have not gotten far with finite understanding yet, considering the fact that we don't know how to live decently with each other. Malice, greed, spite, envy, and all the cruelties incident to these attitudes of individualistic vision, are common, even among the highly literate; and the sufferings of men on this planet, as a direct result of the blindness of men, is so great that a sudden complete sense of it would doubtless ruin any mind. We must widen the range of humanly accredited reality.

To this end we must begin with what we can agree to call known, and here modern psychology comes to our aid. If we know anything, we know that there is a very wide range of sane conscious states; and we know further, when we come to think of it, that *we Occidentals habitually act upon the unconsidered conviction that there is only one valid state—the ordinary waking state.* But even what is generally regarded as the one valid state by which everything is to be tested for reality and valued, has never long remained the same in human history. The standardized state in which a given society tends to appraise all things amounts to no more than the social psychosis of the time; and in our time that psychosis is materialistic in character and physical science is central in it. Or call it a social persuasion based upon a fixed spontaneous attention that excludes in tendency all but a certain single aspect of the world.

When I speak of conscious states, I shall mean nothing in any sense supernatural, but merely "degrees of consciousness," to use the phrase of James Ward—differences in awareness, which everyone experiences, to a greater or less extent, not only in passing from waking into drowse and from drowse into deep sleep, but even when one deems himself broad awake. Everyone has experienced profound changes of mood that seemed to make the world over, either for joy or sorrow. One has not been very observing who does not realize that the world, as we know it, is very largely subjective. Who has not felt a familiar landscape go strange, though every hill and tree and valley remained the same as of old? The pain of loss may change the very look of one's home, until the once friendly lilac bush on the lawn becomes a stranger. For we realize through our sense of relations, and a change of consciousness is a shifting of the focus of spontaneous attention, suppressing the sense of some relations, intensifying the sense of others, or revealing new relations. It is probable that in some people consciousness shifts relatively little, except in sleep; and in others we know that the range is very wide—so wide that the further reaches are generally discredited, since few experience them.

It is the well-established fact of expansive consciousness, as elaborated by F. W. H. Myers, later by James, and more recently to another purpose by Freud, Jung and many others, that corresponds with the essential Vedantist conception of those "stages" whereby the self may rise to disillusionment. Within the range that alone need interest us, the difference is merely one of terminology. Our Brahmin friend, as we have noted, described but three stages; but we know that between these the gradation is continuous, and that the states that may be experienced are not to be numbered; nor is it possible to draw a line at any point below which materialistic science is a valid means of knowing and above which another mode of knowing becomes authoritative. The division is a penumbral region, the exploration of which has only recently begun. Bráhman, we have noted, seems originally to have meant "that which breaks forth, whether in the shape of thought and word or in the shape of creative power or physical force," a conception which perfectly tallies with the modern conception of the subliminal, or ultraliminal, or subconscious, as based upon experiment. We do not follow Myers and the other psychical researchers in their efforts to relate the subliminal in Man to the cosmic. If such relations could be established, the correspondence of Western psychological knowledge with Eastern metaphysical dogma might be made perfect throughout, even to the most profound conception of Bráhman. But we are leaving speculation to the speculators, and we accept the subliminal only in so far as we know it to be a revealing faculty in ourselves and other men, though it may well be more. We cling to the finite, being convinced that the infinite should be big enough to take care of itself, and that if we are able to live in the widest range of humanly intelligible reality our relations with the Whole, whatever that may mean, will be satisfactory. The Whole, to us, must mean all men and what is humanly knowable now. As we proceed we shall hope to find that our acceptance of the fact of expansive consciousness necessarily involves the same essential attitude toward materialism and individualism—those social diseases of the West—that was held by our Brahmin friend; that the application of the fact does not result in a denial of the world in which we live; rather, it greatly extends and glorifies that world; that such an acceptance, far from resulting in a pessimistic negation, will inevitably destroy the foundation for the pessimism of materialism, substituting the melioristic affirmation of a wider range of reality, continuous with that upon which our world now bases its activities. All the world that we know or can know is to be known through our consciousness of relations. Since human consciousness is expansive, we may be certain that a single state—and that approximately the lowest in which men may live and do as men—cannot include all humanly knowable relations; that many states can be aware of more than can one state; that the wider the range of relations we know, the larger shall be our effective world—and the saner and the kinder. We may make a simple picture of the idea by saying that the view of a landscape from a given hilltop is no false view so long as the partial nature of it is understood; for it does reveal some true relations of the landscape. Neither is a view from an airplane a false view, so long as the fact of partiality is considered; and the same may be said of any possible view from any direction. The synthetic view would be the thing to strive for, nevertheless, if an understanding of the landscape were of vital importance to the various spectators. There is a valid common-sense view of the world, and there are also other valid views, and each, though partial, is important. But each is most valuable as a phase of the synthetic view, which can be approximated only by taking into account the whole range of human consciousness.

We may now apply the fact of expansive consciousness to physical science, which is the method by which relations of the common-sense waking state are apprehended to the exclusion of all other possible relations that are to be apprehended through the outer states, which are those of art and poetic values.

However science may be regarded by the mellower seers among its devotees, it has wrought upon the mood of our time as a powerful dogma, well calculated to flatter and convince the many for whom the lure of animality was always a trifle more than a match for the lure of spiritual glory; a dogma that offered a welcome release from the apparently artificial restraints of the higher striving. For the dogma was materialism—a conception that was old in the world, having existed in various forms in the minds of various thinkers since pre-Socratic antiquity, but now entering the general consciousness in an unphilosophical form as a dominant factor in the conduct of life. As scientific materialism, it was the theory that the universe could be explained in terms of matter and motion, the former conceived as the substance of our common-sense world,

the latter as an infinite varying of relationship between the ultimate particles of matter, resulting in
all forms and all phenomena, even consciousness being the result of physical and chemical changes in a
complicated matter-pattern called the nervous system. Anything not physical could not be real, and
the term physical meant the substance of the common-sense world as known to the waking state.
Science would be wholly objective in its methods.
But, our Brahmin friend would ask at this point,
could it be objective, since consciousness was only a
condition of matter? That is to say, the thing
examined was itself the examiner—a state of affairs
with which one could scarcely associate the word
objective. With virtually little more knowledge of
consciousness than the fact of its existence, science
accepted it as a dependable means of knowing reality
through five senses, the mechanism of which it does
not yet understand, for the process by which sense
perception becomes idea is still a mystery. Here
common sense would maintain that science was compelled to begin somewhere; and that had it begun
by studying consciousness, with practically no technique for the task, we might still be rambling about
in the darkness of the older superstitions, the hopeless victims of those natural forces with which we

must live. Since a beginning had to be made, it was best to begin with what we seemed to know, however the search might ultimately prove us to have been mistaken. And this is true.

Nevertheless it was with a sublime act of faith that the faith-destroyer set forth in quest of truth, jauntily packing a load of gratuitous assumption sufficiently great to make even an inspired religion puff and groan on the steeper grades. But science, in the modern sense, was young, and it had one fact upon which it could depend, one fact that obligingly stood still in all the dizzy flux of things, an enormous advantage in a world so suspiciously like a dream. Matter-in-motion was that fact.

Without questioning the proposition that any extended search for reality must, sooner or later, be concerned with the states in which it is apprehended, one not only admits, but insists that this system of relations which is of the animal world and which science has explained in terms of matter moving, most certainly does condition the whole range of animal activity. However these appearances of a limiting solidity might seem to dissolve as shadows for another state, another focus of attention, it remains true that for the state in which men, as mere animals, beget and are born, eat, drink, toil and die, this system of relations is actual and immediate, and the penalty of denial is not to be denied. It would seem that the error of the dogmatic materialist lay in the assumption of a single, unshifting focus of attention, a single constant state of awareness, limited to that one set of relations with which animal existence is obviously concerned. A man viewing a landscape from a given hilltop, and assuming that to be the only viewpoint, could systematize his knowledge of the relations of the landscape. One might insist upon possible views from other hills without questioning the accuracy of the man on the one hill; and if mankind lived by far the greater portion of life on that one hill, the classified knowledge of relations as viewed from that hill would be of enormous importance; and mankind is doing just that.

But if materialistic science was proceeding upon an inadequate assumption in its quest of the livable truth, how can its success be explained? By examining and interpreting the nature of its success, something which the great mass has never done and could hardly be expected to do.

At the outset physical science accepted the world of appearances on the animal level as being real, which, from our viewpoint, was right; and pro-

ceeded to examine that aspect of the world in the
avowed belief that here could be found the whole
of reality, which, from our viewpoint, was wrong.
The real, as Planck, the famous physicist, has said,
"is that which can be measured," either in extension or degree. Science described the appearances,
greatly extended their range within the limits of the
exclusive view, sought for relations between them
and for principles of recurrence whereby other appearances might be predicted. All this being done
with strict reference to one state, the one focus of
attention to which such appearances belonged, it
is easy to see why the theory triumphed, as it did.
Having been made to fit one set of relations, it
could not fail to fit that one set. The fact that it
worked did not prove that the conception was
universally correct, as all scientists know, but as
the great mass of laymen does not know. If it
were not true that a false hypothesis can lead to
valuable results, there could have been no civilization. Also, if hypotheses did not tend to harden
into dogmas, we should probably be more civilized
than we are. If truth is to be likened to the relations of a flowing stream, a dogma is a block of ice
formed from the stream. We are always stopping
and saying: "Here on this height of time we can

see clearly how wrong men have been and now, at last, we are wise"; forgetting that we are the mentally blind ancestors of our posterity, quite as truly as though we had already been dead a thousand years.

And so materialistic science triumphed, a fact for which no thinker, seeing beyond the moment, can be ungrateful. For surely that aspect of the landscape by which animal activity is conditioned was in a sorry mess. Disadvantageous relations had been assumed, and it was by those relations that men must conduct the immediate business of living. Also there were ossified guesses and fantastic taboos that had become as dear as they were detrimental to the slow unfolding of the mind of Man. These guesses were attacked, those relations made more livable. It was not strange that men were profoundly impressed by the doings of this audacious young giant that overthrew the elder gods, performed such miracles as were never seen before, and, parting the shadows of a world conceived as static, revealed a universe of endless change and endless distance with no friend in sight. Men, as always, mistook a dogma for religion, and with the weakening of the dogma it seemed to many that religion was dying. It was not easy to discredit the new doctrine of science in view of the miracles it performed. New dynamic patterns of matter were discovered and made useful; various modes of motion were harnessed and set to work. The whole life of Man on the animal level was greatly emphasized and facilitated, though naturally there were by-products of a higher nature. We have learned how to fly and are greatly excited about it, but it is probable that the gray goose and crane are not greatly impressed. We have made boats that can dive and swim fathoms deep. Thus we have entered into competition with the whale, to the end that we may sneak upon our fellow-men and slay them in the dark. We can talk to each other across seas and continents, but the gabble of a goose will travel by the same means quite as readily as the syllables of a seer. We can travel at speeds that arouse our admiration, but in the end we merely get somewhere else, and generally we start right back at a high rate of speed. The degree of the going is altered, but not the quality of that which goes. The same point can be made throughout the whole range of applied science. Its triumphs, in the main, have been over the environment of essentially brute existence, however disguised. This is a great deal, but it is much less than most men believe. It is altogether possible to live the ethical life of swine while enjoying all of the vaunted blessings of materialistic science. We know this to be true, because it is being done on a vast scale with conspicuous success. A means of rapid communication is valuable if something worthy is communicated. The printing press is valuable in proportion as it prints something humanly worthy. Why do we save labor—to the end that laborers and their families may go hungry? Why fight tuberculosis in the slums—that the number of those who live the lives of rats may not dwindle? For what are they to live? Would it not be less Quixotic to let them die if we have nothing to give them for which to live? Why do we not do this? Hyslop once suggested the answer, and it seems a good one.[1] Whereas science had failed to discover any trace of what had been called soul, there was really nothing left but the body to cherish, and this became automatically the object of man's highest regard—a fact which one may see demonstrated in many ways. In general, the old spiritual priesthood was replaced, in fact, if not in theory, by the new priesthood of medicine; and this statement need not be taken as discrediting either. Anyone is familiar with the sense of credulous awe

[1] *Contact With the Other World.*

that is felt in the presence of the family physician, and there is probably a hidden significance in the fact that the nurse is so often described as an angel of mercy. But even in this prevailing attitude toward the body there is tragi-comedy. Science saves thousands upon thousands of bodies, yet the bland cruelties of our barbaric social system continue; and periodically we destroy human bodies in wholesale quantities by strictly scientific methods. For that which we love most we desire to possess, and when the highest values generally recognized in practice are those of the brute level, we will struggle for those values in the appropriate manner of the brute.

It may be said that physical science has achieved a more than papal authority by virtue of its wonder-working and the strategic position it has won in its duel with an older faith. What it has not proven is widely assumed to be false or doubtful to the point of negligibility—a curious form of logic, as F. W. H. Myers once observed.[1] Its announcements of new theories and new discoveries are immediately accepted by the average layman on faith; and what to scientists themselves is only working hypothesis, seeps into the general consciousness as established

[1] *Science and a Future Life.*

[43]

and marvelous fact, becoming a part of the structure of the world. Anyone must have noted how many minor scientific theories are constantly being announced—theories soon forgotten along with other fads; and yet how readily and with what amazing credulity they are caught up into the goose-gabble of the world! Theory after theory may be discarded, as newly discovered relations render them untenable, and yet the next theory is swallowed by the great mass of laymen without even a query for a chaser and without a bat of the eye. What, at its source, is well known to be only a practicable guess, nicely fitted to the stock of ideas on hand, operates vaguely, but none the less powerfully, in the minds of the mass as a further proof of the omnipotence of science. We who can know nothing of the doings of electrons can, nevertheless, see their infinitely minute solar systems with a vividness unsurpassed by any beatific vision of old. Certainly I can see them now. I could see them plainly before the *Scientific American* furnished me with exact pictures of them; and I am not presuming even to question the theory, for the hypnosis of infallible authority has gripped me too. I am only saying that we laymen still believe what we are told to believe, and that we believe it on faith, just as we believed the older revelations. If this lay attitude were no more than a matter of believing or not believing, it could be treated as amusing by our betters; for this extreme credulity is accompanied by a dogged insistence upon proof for everything. It is a major point of mass etiquette these days to proclaim that we are all from the state of mind called Missouri, and that we are far too knowing to accept anybody's wooden money. But the trouble goes deeper than amusement. This blind faith in a single way of thinking that automatically limits reality to the sensible plane, operates to reassure the brute instincts and tends to limit the whole scale of recognized values to the economic realm. Many deplore this result by formula, but few admit the meaning of it into their lives; most could not even if they would, so great is the economic pressure that would have to be resisted. It is the sort of thing a preacher is expected to discuss on Sunday. He discusses it and then he pronounces the benediction and then we go home to eat or sleep. There is a time and place for everything, we believe; and the place for "lofty" sentiments is in church and the time is Sunday. We are always straddling some imaginary but nevertheless very embarrassing fence. It is not that we are hypocrites necessarily. Such contradictory attitudes are not to be described in all cases by demeaning epithets. We are, for the most part, simply unconscious of the dislocation of the religious sense, and we may be true men—true to our genuine belief. But it is an old and true saying that sincerity is a relative virtue, depending entirely for its worth upon the nature of that about which we are sincere. Hogs fighting for the swill are quite sincere—no less so than men gambling for wealth on the stock exchange. Men shelling and gassing and bayonetting each other for economic advantage are quite sincere—sincere in that state of fixed attention for which such values are omnipotent—so sincere that they glorify their unhuman purpose with a halo of the best they can invent.

It is fortunately true that there is a vast amount of haphazard kindliness in the world, for without it as a mitigating circumstance we could not live at all. And, after all, there is no class to blame; for as a mass we are asleep in a hypnotic suggestion as to the limits of reality, though many of us, reacting to the shock of exterior stimuli that we can neither deny nor prove, toss at the rim of waking and cry out against the idiotic dream. And this conception is more than a figure of speech, for in many ways the moods of the mob—and we are all of it, however much we might sometimes wish to escape—are suspiciously like the phenomena of hypnosis. In this suspicion a hope is revealed; for where a detrimental suggestion can hold despotic sway, a beneficial one may conceivably conquer by the same mechanism. All the kindliness in the world is practically futile so long as it operates within, and in keeping with, the prevailing view of life—a fact which explains the Sisyphean nature of organized charity; also, the tragedy of good intentions in the field of political and social reform. Every four years we become greatly agitated over what are made to appear profound principles, each of which, according to the various expounders, is certain to save us and certain to ruin us. We do not suspect that both of the alleged principles are themselves of the very stuff of the trouble, and that we might vote and shout ourselves into a state of collapse—as we very nearly do—without touching the source of the trouble, so long as the ideas attacked and defended are themselves formed out of the view that hurts us. What matter which wins, since in either case, as a social body, we continue to sleep the sleep of the brute, in kind though not in degree? Why develop a more efficient technique for doing precisely that which hurts us? It is the method of one who fights shadows in a dream, unaware that there is a dream and that the shadows are of it.

It should be asked here: If we grant that we are hypnotized by the facts of a single focus of attention, how may we describe a social waking state, since each new focus, according to the contention, would induce merely a different dream? The answer, in keeping with our view, is that we sleep to the greater portion of what is humanly knowable and necessary; and that a correlation of the values of all human states of awareness—judged for validity by their effects upon the lives of men— would, for us, be an awakening out of illusion. To put the idea into modern psychological terms, we may say that the general consciousness of our time is suffering from dissociation.

It will be noted that while this view is based upon the Oriental pattern, it is not Oriental idealism. It is merely an extended realism, based upon the conception of an ascending scale of consciousness, which is a fact even within the narrow limits of the brute realm, as one may learn by associating with a cow. On the other hand, it might be said that I merely insist upon the obvious, the fact of an ascending scale of consciousness being well known. But if the fact were given any practical significance, it would not be considered possible to educate a human being on one level only—and more and more just that is being done. We must believe this so long as it is possible to meet graduates who have no acquaintance with the higher levels, and accredited educators with the minds of calico clerks.

If it were possible for a man to exchange ideas with a cat while in the dizzy act of chasing its tail, we may be sure that the cat would consider the man a hopeless visionary for contending that the tail could never be overtaken. The cat would know well enough that the proper way to overtake any escaping object is to increase the speed of pursuit. (That is what our civilization is constantly doing.) The cat might lay great stress on the technique of pursuit, thus winning much applause from strictly scientific cats. We learn from the psychology of dreaming that any train of argument conceived in a given state is convincing for that state, and that it is only on the troubled border of change from one state to another that the force of the argument can be doubted; only in another state that it can be rejected. Then how can our fragmentary dreams be clarified and fused into a livable conception of Man and the world?

Our institutions, to which we once looked for leadership on the higher levels, now seem all but powerless to help, for the great hypnosis grips them too; and when, as from the silent places of the future, one listens for the humanizing music of the wider life from a thousand seats of learning, one hears, for the most part, a sound most distressingly like a snore—or is it only the roaring of the stadium? Barbaric hordes, asserting the divine right of democracy, have broken into the temples, guffawing and profane and certain of their power. And it would be well if it were the hordes that were raised, but it is the temple that changes. For these, in the main, do not come asking humbly to be lifted out of the animal view of life. "Make us more efficient animals," they cry, "that we may hope to glut ourselves at the rich troughs of the world." And it is a pitiful cry; for back of it somewhere is the ancient fear of hunger, not yet conquered for all our vaunted cleverness in handling material things; and nearer is the old pathetic desire to be envied. Such an attitude on the part of students is to be expected in a society that tends to state all values in terms of brute measurement. It is a common thing nowadays to hear of the cash value of "an education." Note the use of the article, *"an* education," as though education were something detached from the proprietor—a piece of property! Statisticians, by way of inducing the young person to get one of these desirable pieces of property for himself, have shown the exact cash value of a college education, which is more expensive than the grade school or high school brand. One page of an arithmetic text studied by my children is devoted to that sort of thing. I do not remember the figure, and I think it does not make much difference. Let us assume that a college education of the best and most widely advertised brand is worth exactly $62,500 on the world market. Of course there are cheaper brands, but this is a quality article. Now let us see what this means. Not many years ago one Jack Dempsey knocked down one Carpentier eight times, receiving for his toil a half million of these standard units of universal value called dollars. For every manly wallop he landed on the Frenchman he received $62,500. During my most impressionable years I was told that things equal to the same thing are equal to each other, and I cannot forget the statement. Therefore a college education of the best and most widely advertised brand is exactly equivalent to a good stiff wallop on the jaw, and Carpentier received the equivalent of eight distinct college educations from Doctor Dempsey in exactly 3 minutes and 49 seconds.

I have met many teachers in many schools and colleges who seemed to be awake. But it is only human to remember that to shout too obstreperously into the ear of a surly and powerful sleeper is to get kicked unceremoniously out of bed; and one does not deny the reality of brute necessities, nor the need to be respected by one's fellow-men. One merely insists upon the importance of *human* values.

A great deal of adverse criticism is being heaped upon our schools. They are being blamed for materialistic tendencies. But a school is a human institution, serving as the society, that has created it, demands that it shall serve. It is the flow of life that determines the forms of life, and the school is a form determined by the flow of prevailing ideas. Only a change in the flow can break down old forms and make new. The critics of schools should attack the materialistic psychosis of society, and be certain, while doing so, that they themselves are not in the grip of the materialistic dream in the form of abject money-awe.

Meanwhile, it is possible for the superior student to question as to whether or not a life spent in getting a living, or even the equivalent of ten thousand livings, is worth a single pang of longing. By seriously considering the question it is possible to experience a change of attitude that will seem little short of miraculous, for thereby the whole world will become new. Some idea of such a transformation may be given by citing the familiar example of the changing cube. Represent a transparent cube by drawing the twelve lines of its edges. First fix your attention on the front line of the bottom face, and notice the position of the whole figure. Then transfer the focus of your attention to the back line of the bottom face. Suddenly the cube will turn inside out; the back line of the bottom face will be the front line, and the figure will have changed its position in space. This is called an optical illusion. Nevertheless, it is, in a small way, a change of consciousness. The altered relation of the two lines proves nothing against the order of ideas that we may let the first front line represent; but it proves something in favor of the order of ideas that we may let the former back line represent. We do not leap to the conclusion that the back line was always the front line, or vice versa. The same transformation is possible with all lines of the cube, and all views of it are certainly true, but only as each is related to the other views. The materialist, fixing his attention on one line, sees a hard and changeless body. The idealist sees only shifting illusions within the self. *The synthetic realist would see the cube living in all its relations.*

Many in all classes are doubtless either awake or near enough to the borders of waking to suspect that there is a dream and that it is absurd. May it not be that it is within this troubled margin of the broken sleep that so many fantastic modern social and religious cults originate, like presentative dreams that attempt an explanation of exterior stimuli? Like a vast spectrum, this sense of a despotic folly cuts in delicately shaded bands of awareness directly across the horizontal stratification of our materialistic society; and it is in this gradation of understanding that we might look for the dynamic pattern of a sane social order based upon a full recognition of the whole range of the man, the whole scale of humanly realizable values from lowest to highest.

And how is a movement to be started in the direction of such a social conception? By thinking about it, first of all. Certainly nothing can be done by passing laws that must be formed out of the very stuff of the offending psychosis. It may be that we shall have to wait for economic processes to reach that point of negation and consequent catastrophe which seems inevitable in our fragmentary conception of Man. We seemed very near such a breakdown during the great war, and there has been no shifting of the general attention since then. We did not like the war, because it hurt us. We did not seem to know, and do not yet, that we were fighting the objective representation of our own individualistic obsession; and, accordingly, many of us have hit upon the brilliant idea of arriving at a gentleman's agreement to the end that hereafter the painful effect shall not follow the cause. It is the fantastic method of a dream in which the fundamental assumption is not questioned except on the border of waking. But if, as a result of general economic breakdown and widespread woe, the present mood of society should be replaced by an anti-materialistic one, the reaction would probably be in the direction of a savage supernaturalism; for the mass knows nothing of that direction perpendicular to the axis of opposites whereby the livable truth is wont to escape us. It knows only to stampede toward the opposite extreme from that which hurts it.

Perhaps there is hope in the fact that many individuals grow weary of the dream, though they may believe that their weariness is with life itself. Surely it seems that society is in a highly suggestible state at present. Anywhere a new contagion might begin and sweep the world as the crossword puzzle craze has done. The change should not come spontaneously from the mass, but from those who, by virtue of a more inclusive range of values, are at least able to point the direction. This is more than a matter of formal scholarship; for it is conceivable that a man might have systematic knowledge of all human value-forms without vitalizing any but those of the lower range; and it is a fact that learning displays a strong tendency to become negative. Thought-forms become inflexible, checking the creative flow that made them; and the forms are held long after the creative flow has turned elsewhere. The very rigidity of such forms is certain to inspire confidence in the average mind, which is always longing for permanence, conceived, not as direction, but as immobility.

Perhaps the most compelling hope is to be found in the present trend of scientific theory. This involves a point at which we have been aiming while we have been trying to determine how extensive the truth of common sense may be. We have been noting how the scientific materialist assumed that all reality could be found within a certain focus of attention comprehending relations described as physical. The realm in which he proposed to find the explanation of all phenomena coincided with the realm of common sense, the values thereof being only quantitatively extended. But man is the artist animal, which is to say that his consciousness is expansive. The very fact of the materialist's profound absorption in his scientific problem signified the passing of the ordinary state, the shifting of the focus with reference to which his theory was necessarily conceived.

If a given man in his ordinary moods lived in a field of attention coinciding exactly with that of his horse, and if the man should undertake to explain his world with reference to that single focus of attention, his attempt would seem altogether commendable to the horse, for he would be acting in keeping with horse sense. But however the man might believe the limitations of his own consciousness to be those of his equine friend, the fact would be different. The man would be using human consciousness, capable of considerable expansion, in his explanation of the horse's world; and the disparity between horse- and man-consciousness would be revealed in apparent contradictions. It might not at once be clear to the man where the difficulty lay, and he might easily bridge embarrassing gaps in his thought by creating unintelligible symbols, which would work well enough in his horse-sense theories for awhile. But if the man were to continue his inquiry logically, he would arrive sooner or later at a seeming negation of the whole world. Thereupon a horse of a certain temperament might leap to the conclusion that the world is merely one's idea;[1] and a persuasive horse religion might be founded upon that conclusion. Nevertheless, the horse's world would remain a scientific fact, as any horse might prove by attempting to live on metaphysical pasture and purely conceptual water. The man's inquiry would have proven merely, what should have been obvious to the man, that the relations known to the horse could not be expected to explain the world of larger relations that a man may know. Neither set of relations would be repudiated thus. The human world-view would be to the horse world-view what our poetry is to our science; and the difference involved would be concerned with something far more important, in the

[1] Here I borrow from Ouspensky, cited in the prefatory note, in so far as the discrepancy between the conceptions of animal and human consciousness is concerned. He, however, reaches the conclusion of our hypothetical horse in the manner indicated.

conduct of horse life, than mere factual knowledge. (Proceeding upward in the scale of consciousness, is it not at least conceivable that beings beyond men may regard our poetry as we our science; that is to say, as the fundamental mode of thought by which the new frontier of understanding is to be approached?)

Similarly, the scientific materialist had been able to establish the wave-like motion of light as a working conception; yet light waves found no difficulty in passing through a vacuum. Already the idea of motion in nothing had been approached, whereas motion in matter was the prime essential. But in keeping with the commonsense focus of attention, a something called æther was invented as a convenient medium for the propagation of light waves. This was a practical thing to do, and ever since æther was invented, light waves have been using it regularly in their cosmic business of illumination.

The method thus employed by way of upholding a theory reminds one of Lewis Carroll's method of writing poetry. Assuming a certain mood, for which appropriate material was not available, he managed to maintain the mood by inventing unintelligible sounds to bridge the gaps between his intelligible words.

" 'Twas brillig, and the slithy toves
  Did gyre and gimble in the wabe——"

We know, of course, that æther is accepted merely as a necessary working symbol of the unknown; but what if the inquiry be pushed so far that nothing but such symbols remain? So long as matter itself did not run away and hide beyond finding, the cosmic game of hide-and-seek could proceed according to the established rules. For so long as there was matter to cling to, it was possible to ignore all phenomena that could not, apparently, be described as physical in any accepted scientific sense. Orthodox science has done that and is still doing it. It has clung to its original negative assumption, refusing to consider all phenomena apparently related to the mystery of human personality, limiting its psychology to pure mechanism, and even seeking the origin of mind in muscular reactions. Science has been like a lawyer defending a client and using only evidence favorable to his case. There are, doubtless, many scientists who can say truthfully, slightly altering the words of Shandy to my Uncle Toby: "Materialism was my aunt, but Truth is my sister;" and any one of those could give many instances of this disparity between the unfolding conceptions of an expanding consciousness and the

[60]

preconception of a lower state regarded as the only valid one. But in view of the development of scientific thought in recent years, a complete catalogue of such disparities is unnecessary.

There are two generally accepted directions in which we fancy that the fleeing shadow of truth may be pursued across the plane of awareness which is concerned with our ordinary world of animal existence—toward the very, very large and toward the very, very small. We are pitifully obsessed with such exclusively quantitative conceptions. Science has proceeded in both directions. Proceeding in the direction of the inconceivably small, it arrived, unexpectedly, but by the compelling logic of experiment, at a new conception of the atom, which was formerly conceived as the ultimate division of matter. It is now persuaded by its own logic to conceive the atom as a minute solar system of electrons revolving about a nucleus of positive electricity, the electrons being point charges of negative electricity. But electricity is not to be conceived as matter. It is to be conceived, somehow, as motion. Of the twofold fact assumed by science —matter-in-motion—it would seem that matter has disappeared and only motion remains. Motion in what? An idealistic monist would insist that it is motion in universal consciousness, and that the illusory nature of the empirical world is thus revealed; but we are not led to this conclusion. This is the same poser that little Alice faced in Wonderland when she saw the grinning cat slowly fade away until nothing but the grin was left. Alice marveled at the phenomenon, remarking that she had often seen a cat without a grin, but never a grin without a cat. Her difficulty, according to our view, lay in the fact that she had taken the familiar standards of waking into Wonderland, where she could never have arrived had the waking state been the only possible one. Obviously, her only hope was in awakening to the necessity of examining her consciousness; but Alice, being a Victorian, was nothing if not scientific and altogether practical. There may well be a sense in which motion-in-nothing, to use our crude terms, is a reality; but it is certainly not in the sense upon which scientific materialism has based its whole structure. It is in the unlivable Oriental sense.

That the conception of motion-in-nothing has been faced by science was shown a quarter of a century ago in Thompson's elaboration of the electronic theory; for Thompson described electrons as probably being "centres of self-locked and permanent strain existing in the universal æther," æther being a name for the unknown. Surely this is getting rather far from common sense. Bertrand Russell, after a lucid and wholly sympathetic explanation of the whole theory, has lately remarked that æther, after all, may be what is really fundamental; that is to say, it is the unknown that is fundamental after all.

Since we are led by what we believe to be logical means to the conception of nothing in motion, why not accept spiritual monism? The difference is only in words which, in either case, are empty except as emotion may fill them—a state of affairs against which modern science was a most commendable revolt.

But also science has proceeded in the direction of the inconceivably large, and has come by logical experiment to the principle of relativity. As the electronic theory works in chemistry, so does the theory of relativity work not only in the realm of the inconceivably large but in the realm of the inconceivably small as well. Outside the great works of pure literature I think I have read nothing that has thrilled me more than this particular chapter in the history of thought. Moritz Schlick,[1] one of the

[1] Schlick: *Space and Time in Contemporary Physics.*

abler exponents of the new conception, shows how "the theory of relativity entirely does away with the traditional conceptions of space and time, and banishes æther as a substance out of physics." What we now have of the materialistic universe is merely an electromagnetic field in a vacuum, all forms and all phenomena being merely disturbances in this electromagnetic field. "We must be very careful, however," warns Professor Schlick, "not to picture it as matter."

We may quote Russell [1] again by way of showing the healthy state of uncertainty in which science now finds itself. After uttering a word of warning against a too ready acceptance of present scientific theories, he says: "It should not be forgotten that there is another order of ideas, temporarily out of fashion, which may at any moment come back into favor. . . . It is plausible to suppose that every apparent law of nature which strikes us as reasonable is not really a law of nature but a concealed convention plastered on to nature by our love of what we, in our arrogance, choose to consider rational." Eddington, quoted by Russell, suggests "that a real law of nature is likely to stand out by the fact that it appears to us irrational, since in that

[1] Russell: *The A B C of Atoms.*

Note : -

case it is less likely that we have invented it to satisfy our intellectual taste." Thus even the rational process, upon which the whole structure of scientific thought has been based, begins to seem doubtful. Surely Science, which is Common Sense in long pants, seems to have wandered beyond the limits of its home town and finds the customs strange!

If it be true that human consciousness is expansive—and this is hardly to be doubted so long as seers and dolts exist together, even if the fact had not been established by psychology—then it is necessary to infer that the wider state will include the more; and when men attempt an explanation of the humanly realizable world from the facts of a single focus of attention, every hypothesis they may advance must lead them to negation. It is no more than a matter of exclusive spontaneous attention, and it will make no difference what focus is assumed to be the only dependable one—that of the dogmatic materialist or that of the dogmatic idealist. Beginning with either, regarded as exclusive, men will arrive at emptiness. Have not certain scientific thinkers done that; and is there not something pathetic in their attempts to conjure a conveniently finite universe by means of the conception of curved space? As though a finite universe were easier to understand than an infinite universe! In one case all ends are endless, and in the other, endlessness somehow ends.

Does it not seem that truly a very different order of ideas is needed? Why not explore human personality and get acquainted with the Knower? Is is not reasonable to think that science, in order to preserve its character as a distinctive way of thinking, and an absolutely necessary one, must sooner or later, in its advanced form, become the science of human personality, throwing away the negative assumption that now embarrasses it, and regarding physical science as an efficient servant on the animal level only? The development of the diatonic scale through the circle of keys in music furnishes a good picture of such a progression to higher beginnings through cycles of apparent defeat. Starting with the scale of C, each successive scale, based on the dominant tone of the last, increases regularly the number of its sharps until six are reached in the scale of F sharp. Thereupon, by way of avoiding an embarrassing complexity, the equivalent six flats are substituted, these decreasing regularly in number in each successive scale until the scale of C is reached again—a return to the simplicity of the starting point, but with the difference that the pitch is higher. If the range of the piano were very great, a very great number of such cycles could be assumed. To apply the analogy, we may suggest that science has passed through one cycle of its diatonic scale, apparently arriving again at the point from which it set out. *But the pitch is higher;* and to proceed as science, to escape the danger of becoming art, must it not acknowledge the necessity of the raised pitch? Here one might say that if each C scale, pitched higher than the last, is made to signify a new and subtler hypothesis, leading only to another return, what could be the justification of seeking to know at all? Nothing but the exploration of human consciousness. Is not that enough for us? And who else is concerned? Somehow our salvation is within us.

With the wonderful technique for inquiry that science has developed in its ascent from the brute levels, it might well be expected to reveal in no doubtful manner new vistas of truth that would make its former miracles seem mere entertainment for babes—or brutes. And by the very fact of its position of authority on the lower levels, it might well revolutionize the whole life of Man, shifting the social center of gravity in the direction of those higher values which alone can justify our being born and eating and drinking and toiling and dying. This shifting of the spontaneous attention of the world would occur automatically, however slowly; for the foundations of our limiting conception of the world of men would be swept away by the very mode of thought that has authorized the conception and made it practically omnipotent. The new science would certainly be more than psychology as we use the term now, and its purpose would be to enlarge our world qualitatively as well as quantitatively, building a way across the gap which so many are constantly leaping in a pathetic attempt to keep alive in one world for the sake of another and very different one. This gap is represented in modern thinking by the gulf that separates physics from psychology. The problem of showing that it may be only a band of shadow has already been experimentally attacked with promising results, notably by Doctor Crawford of Glasgow University,[1] who is neither a poet nor a metaphysician, but a mechanical engineer, unhampered, however, by any set notion as to the necessary limitations of the real. The problem of dissolving that shadow is of immeasurably greater importance than all the other problems about which there is constantly so much

[1] *The Reality of Psychic Phenomena.*

palaver among the mighty. A solution of this particular problem could not give us any ultimate conception of the universe; but a solution would tend to establish the unbroken relationship of the higher and lower fields of human attention with their corresponding values from lowest to highest within our human limitations, definitely authorizing and vitalizing the whole chain of possible human experience, so that men might no longer look upon the upper range of values as mere emotional luxury or as an imaginative means of temporary escape from reality, but as the very stuff of reality more vividly perceived by virtue of larger relations—quite as much the stuff of human life as food and water and air are the stuff of brute life.

A quarter of a century ago Frederick Myers pointed out what is still an astonishing fact, that there never has been any certain classified knowledge of human personality and the means by which it is constantly operating. Men have studied the mechanism of thought, which is a very different matter, and the whole subject of human personality, which would seem to be the prime consideration in any attempt to understand the human world, has been left to the jugglers of institutionalized superstition. So long as this field remains virgin to accredited science, we are hardly justified in assuming that the complex structure of the world's learning is well founded.

This hope that is held by many in our time might sound to the common-sense man suspiciously like poetry at best. It *is* poetic in our special sense, as will appear later; nevertheless it is based upon nothing so vague as the average man's conception of poetry; for while orthodox science has been toiling in an exclusive realm, unorthodox science, quite as cautious, quite as methodical and quite as patient as its scornful and myopic cousin, has been piling up a vast mass of observations relative to human personality. It is not to be assumed that anyone can predict just what the new science will find; but enough is known to justify the belief that the old hopelessly limiting notions will be destroyed, and with them, sooner or later, will go the hideous and cruel superstition that we call materialism; and individualism—the acute form of our social disease— is implicit in the materialistic view.

It is encouraging to remember that orthodox and highly accredited thinkers once argued the question as to how many angels might comfortably congregate on the point of a needle, and that the world of laymen did not laugh until the fashion in guesses had changed—that is to say, not until a new suggestion had induced a new world psychosis.

There was once a monster called the Infidel. He, alas, has become dogmatic. Now there must be infidels to materialism in steadily increasing numbers; and in good time, after the new infidel shall have won his fight, he too will become overcertain of his world, dogmatizing the little he can grasp of the new vision. So shall he become, in turn, altogether respectable and useless.

Alas for the searcher after truth who shall fall asleep in the Many!

A little while ago, it was said that a given phase of thought, based upon a single focus of attention, if logically developed, must evolve into a higher phase with the inevitable shifting of the focus, thus escaping at last the realm in which it started. Has science, in its further reaches, crossed the boundaries of the realm of art?

Fancy yourself as going forth some golden day of early spring into a windless forest. You have gone there to chop summer wood, and you are looking for a tree that will make the most satisfactory fuel. You pass the basswoods and the sycamores and even the oaks. You are scientific, and you know that, although oak makes a good fire, hickory is better. You do not fall to chopping the first hickory tree you find, for trees differ in adaptability to your purpose. You want the most wood for the least effort. At last you stand before a hickory that suits your common-sense purpose, and you gaze upward along the bole, noting the soaring taper of it. The place is very quiet, and it may be that your thrifty neighbor would describe you as lazy. Perhaps he would be right, for him. But there is surely a sense in which it is true that by going far one finds nothing and by going fast one overtakes nothing. In fact, you should have been getting up your summer wood during the winter, for the sap has already begun to lift; the maples are oozing; there is a stippling of leaf buds against the blue; soft white clouds go over; a few birds flute and chatter.

Then, if you are a certain sort of person—that is to say, if you are not altogether sense-bound—something wonderful may happen to you. Suddenly the tree, conceived as hickory firewood, fades away. With a timeless sense, in which the very identity of the woodchopper is lost, you may feel the ecstatic upward suck of resurrected life through bole and branch and twig, almost as though the body of the tree were your own. And there will be something very much like love in the sense and something near to happy tears—when it has become a memory. This may pass in a flash, however long the time; but all that day you are likely to be kinder than usual—even to the dogs you may chance to meet. You have felt the larger relations and lost yourself in them.

I have purposely offered an extreme example; but there are those of us who are convinced that the higher vision of the tree is concerned with those values which alone can justify the effort to keep from freezing to death by using the tree as fuel. And it is not only when in contact with what we ordinarily call nature that such a swift change may occur. It may happen in crowded streets at the very moment when you feel most disgusted with the brawling, wriggling mess of humanity and with yourself as a part of it. Here too the sense of love and loss of self may occur. It is the cube of our illustration turning inside out; it is the scientific mood passing without a shock into the poetic.

So it has been in no carping spirit that I have read of these ultra-modern scientific theories. On the contrary, their beauty has moved me deeply, filling me with the old rhythmic sense of awe that has long been the vitalizing force of all my little striving. In moments of intense comprehension, immediately lost, I have felt in them the wingèd symmetries of music, the creative rhythms of the dreaming mind of Man, the glory of the loss of self in dim and vast relations.

Can it be that the poet and the physicist are merged in Bohr and Planck, the poet and the mathematician in Einstein? Is this not inevitable, since they are men? And if the modern theories are not science, but poetry, should we devotees of the poetic values be scornful? Should we not rather rejoice to believe that the old notion of antagonism is an illusion, and that both the scientific and the poetic belong to one flowing circle of *human* reality? And if this be poetry, what is its theme but the ancient longing to know? And the symbols of its expression are the circle in space and time—symbols of human limitation—pictures of the human dream, always essaying an infinite journey and always returning upon itself.

II

THE CREATIVE DREAM

II

THE CREATIVE DREAM

It must have been noted that in using the word poetry I could not have been thinking of that particular literary form which we ordinarily contrast with prose. I was thinking, rather, of a characteristic quality that distinguishes the genuine products of all the arts from the works of pure common sense, however elaborate and imposing they may be. Literary definitions of poetry can be no more than partial descriptions. The definition of poetry must be psychological; it is only verse that can be defined in literary terms.

Of the four arts, sculpture, painting, poetry and music, sculpture is that one which seems to exist wholly in the common-sense world. It is tangible, has length, breadth and thickness. For this reason it may well seem to the average sense-bound man to partake more fully of the nature of reality than do the three others. Sculpture, such a man might say, can be measured and weighed; it is there; it has body; there is no "imagination" about it. This apparent advantage might be made to seem enormous. I once met an enthusiastic lady who emphasized that advantage for my enlightenment. Sculpture was obviously the supreme art, she contended, because it could be made to outlast "the tooth of time and the tongue of fire." It could conceivably be made to outlast the very tenure of man himself on this planet, though what advantage that might be she did not say; and one fears that she might have been puzzled had one chanced to remark that a supreme work of sculpture could be modelled in wax, though wretched examples of the art have certainly been wrought in granite and bronze. The lady had merely confused Geology with Æsthetics in a vague way—nor greatly to her discredit, considering the fact that she was living in a time when it was possible to define the real as that which can be measured, though no one has attempted to compute the horsepower generated by Shelley in his "Ode to the West Wind."

However, as I happened to know, this same lady's spirit was far finer than her understanding; and, to employ a familiar example, had two plaster figures of a girl been placed before her, one having been cast by mechanical means directly from the living body and the other having been modelled by a truly great sculptor, it is not before the first that the lady would have stood the longer to gaze. On the contrary, it is quite probable that the first, for all its marvelous accuracy, would have produced in her a distinctly disagreeable mood; while the second would have induced a state of mind much like that of a dream, an experience not readily to be forgotten for the strange uplift that accompanied it. But if, at the same time, one with no more psychic equipment than is absolutely essential to a butcher should have been examining the two figures, he would very sensibly have chosen the first, and of the second he would have said: "There are no such girls in the world." And he would have been right, since he would have been speaking of the world of a butcher.

Proceeding to the art of painting we find that here one of the dimensions of the common-sense world is lost. Only length and breadth remain; thickness, depth, have become a matter of illusion. One may look behind the picture and he will find nothing there. From the strictly common-sense viewpoint we have taken a step downward in the scale of the Arts, since one-third of painting is "imaginary"; and any practical person knows that to call anything "imaginary" is to wipe it quite out of existence for common sense people, who are wise and shrewd. We know they are wise and shrewd, for it is they who are conducting the business of the world!

Still, there may be a difference in paintings, as in everything else. Two men paint each a picture of an opening in a forest with the sunlight sifting through at a given angle. The first man is a wonderful mechanic, and he paints with photographic accuracy. He paints everything that is to be seen with the eye and he paints nothing that cannot be seen by our hypothetical gentleman whose psychic equipment does not exceed that which is absolutely essential to a butcher. The second painter is George Inness; and it is plain to the butcher that the second picture is inaccurate. No such sunlight ever fell upon his world, and no hog ever nosed about for mast among such queer trees. A hog or a horse or a cow would, no doubt, agree perfectly with the butcher. However, a certain impractical man, with a somewhat different psychic equipment, happens along, and it is before the second picture that he stands and stares in self-forgetfulness. He may even be heard to quote some such queer lines as these by Lanier:

O what if a sound should be made!
O what if a bound should be laid
To this bow-and-string tension of beauty and silence a-spring,
To the bend of beauty, the bow, and the hold of silence,
    the string!

Whereupon the butcher might make his first contribution to Aesthetics, saying: "No wonder that fellow never had a dollar in the bank!"

Passing on to the literary form we call poetry, we find that the common-sense world has been evaporating rather rapidly. We had already lost one dimension in painting, which was alarming enough, but now we seem to have lost the other two—surely a dizzy fall. For certainly a poem cannot be said to have either breadth or thickness; and when one has puzzled over the matter for a little while, one sees that it has not even length in the ordinary way of thinking. For it is not necessary that a poem should be written down or printed in order to be a poem. It may have existed for generations without having been recorded by any material means. One might say that it is to be measured, if at all, by the time required in reciting it aloud or repeating it to oneself; but this method would give us a variable yardstick. Furthermore, it would seem to exist even when not being repeated, else how could one repeat it? But, after all, a poem cannot exist independently of words, and we may count the number of words when we repeat the poem, thus managing to salvage one dimension from the wreck of reality. But, for all its pitiful limitations, this is evidently a most ambitious art; for though it can be measured in only one way, has not weight, and cannot be appraised in terms of energy, it presumes to take not only the whole common-sense world for its province, but deals with that solid, three dimensional world as moving in time, thus adding another measurement to the list of its pretensions; and yet it has only one real dimension to its name.

This art, then, must be largely make-believe—a childish business—and it is therefore not difficult to understand why poets are likely to be somewhat unlike us practical people. No wonder some of them have starved to death in a world of plenty! They have simply failed to understand that "life is real and life is earnest."

Summoning our official æsthetician, the butcher, we find that there is indeed something very wrong about this art, for since his experience with painting he has grown uneasy about the whole subject of art, and he has been looking into the matter.

He is no man of half measures, being accustomed to plunge the knife straight to the gushing heart of things, and he has gone at once to no less a poem than the *Iliad,* for he has been told that this poem was regarded as great even before the Christian Era and is even now held in some esteem in certain quarters. Happily the marvelous prose translation by Lang, Leaf and Myers is available, and very soon this alleged masterpiece hangs eviscerated and open to the light of common sense.

Evidently, as the butcher points out, the *Iliad* was intended to be a sort of history, but such history as only a very childish person could write and only a very young child could believe. The exaggeration, everywhere apparent, is outrageous, and even after one has stripped away all the exaggeration, one finds the subject-matter quite unimportant, even if the Trojan War be accepted as a fact. If a story of war is wanted, why not read about the World War, which really happened, as everybody knows, and was conducted on a scale and with a violence calculated to make the Trojan War look like a kindergarten game?

But at this point someone else begins to speak, as though he hadn't heard the butcher at all, and it is Andrew Lang, and his voice is the voice of countless men through many generations, reaching back to Peisistratus and beyond into that dimmer time when wandering rhapsodists, "sons of Homer, singers of the stitched song," held spellbound groups of half barbaric men. And they are tall words that Andrew Lang is saying, some of which are as follows: "Homer is a poet for all ages, all races and all moods. To the Greeks his epics were not only the best of romances, the richest of poetry; not only their oldest documents about their own history—they were also their Bible, their treasury of religious and moral teaching. There is no good quality that they lack; manliness, courage, reverence for old age and for the hospitable hearth; justice, piety, pity, a brave attitude toward life and death are all conspicuous in Homer. He is the *second-sighted* man. He is universal as humanity, simple as childhood, musical now as the flow of his own rivers, now as the heavy plunging wave of his own Ocean."

Having heard this much, the butcher makes not only his exit but his second contribution to Æsthetics, saying: "Surely these poets and lovers of poetry are sometimes out of their senses!" And this is a true saying, as we shall see; but for reasons unknown to the butcher.

We have now come to music, the last in our scale of arts; and from the standpoint of scientific reality we have come to the jumping off place with nowhere to jump and apparently nothing to jump from. We were safe with sculpture and its three-way solidity. The trouble began when we sacrificed one-third of reality for the art of painting. The situation became alarming when, in descending to poetry, we were hard put to save even one-third of the real; but here in the art of music the situation becomes intolerable. For what shall we say of music as existing in space? We will not push the point involved in the fact that deaf Beethoven could experience a whole sonata without the aid of those disturbances in the air that we call sound; for this would make the case hopeless, and we really do not want to banish music out of the world. Even our friend, the butcher, wants to save music if only it can be done; for some years ago he spent a goodly number of perfectly real dollars for a victrola, and of late he has purchased a radio set. The music of these has seemed real to him heretofore, even quite scientifically so, for he could readily perceive the fact that both these instruments were products of science. But now that he has become a self-conscious critic of the arts, he is greatly troubled.

[85]

First of all, what is the subject matter of music anyway? Sculpture presents an image of something real. Painting, even though it depends upon illusion, gives one a more or less recognizable picture of reality. Poetry, for all its intolerable make-believe, talks about something, however one may feel compelled to reject that something. But what does music talk about? One may fancy that it is telling something, but the man in the next seat fancies something very different. Does it seem to create pictures of reality? But a thousand pictures may be produced thus in a thousand different minds by one musical composition, and no two pictures will be in the least alike, except by accident. Can it be that music has no content that is describable in terms of the real? One may say that it produces patterns in air vibrations; but even so, do such patterns necessarily bear any likeness whatever to any patterns of reality existing in our common-sense world? And if such patterns bear no likeness whatever to anything in our experience, how can we respond to them? Since it is scientific to believe only in a world made wholly of such stuff as hams and Ford cars are made of, and superstitious to believe in any other sort of world, it looks as though the butcher might be compelled, in the interest of sanity, to discard his victrola and use his radio set only as a means of ascertaining the latest quotations on fat hogs. This would be a pity, for heretofore, when he listened to his victrola it was as though something unintelligibly delightful were passing rapidly through the surface of his awareness; but out of what into what, since all practical people know that nothing is real that is not limited to one surface of awareness, if you only push your inquiry far enough?

Indeed, Hugo seems to have been right when he said that "Music is the vapor of Art." Even the butcher is forced to grant that it is surely the most unreal of the arts; and yet this is the only one of the arts that really moves the butcher at all! Though a piece of sculpture or a painting or a poem may leave him unmoved, he can sit for hours listening with unflagging delight to the music of his victrola. Is it possible that we have been descending in the scale of the arts? If we have been descending from the real toward the bottomless abyss of unreality, how can we explain the effect of music upon the butcher, who is nothing if not practical? We have seen him very sensibly rejecting the progressive unreality of the other arts, only to find that the least real of them all is the only one that grips him; and this is due to no idiosyncrasy of the butcher. It is well known that of all the arts music has the widest appeal. Is it barely possible that we have been ascending after all? But how can this be true, since we know, having been told by men far "smarter" than we are, that the real is that which can be measured?

It would be sacrilegious to question this doctrine of the modern materialistic priesthood, just as it was sacrilegious to question the doctrines of an earlier priesthood; so the butcher does not venture to ask if, after all, something important may not have been overlooked in this preoccupation with a certain set of measuring sticks, such as length, breadth, thickness, weight, energy, etc.

Once upon a time a particularly ingenious savage hit upon the idea that everything had extent in three distinct ways, and that he could determine how big everything in his world was by noting how many times he could lay a certain stick down in each direction; and it was no wonder that he came to have a mystical regard for so wonderful a stick, for it told him very much that he needed to know. But when he undertook to determine how many sticks could be laid down between breakfast and supper, he was puzzled. Could breakfast and supper be really one meal, in no way separated except by "imagination"? His stomach scouted the idea; nevertheless the sanctified measuring stick could not be questioned. Had it not performed wonders? Doubtless he brought the matter to the attention of his wife, demonstrating the impossibility of laying the infallible stick in any way whatsoever that would show even the slightest interval between breakfast and supper and arguing cogently that breakfast should therefore be a continuous perform- ance. However, as men in general now agree, women are hopelessly illogical, and one can fancy the savage woman saying: "Get along with your precious stick; there'll be no supper until sundown!" All intuition, you see; absolutely unmoved by the nicest demonstration of reason! It was then, no doubt, that a man remarked for the first time, what countless men have since remarked, that there are occupations more profitable than arguing with one's wife. And what did the savage scientist do then? He continued to regard the magical stick as holy and in no way to be doubted. It became an article of faith with him that breakfast and supper were in no way separated. Nevertheless, he continued to wait for his supper. In the same way, the butcher continues to enjoy the values of music, which cannot be real because they cannot be measured. And scientists themselves have been known to attend concerts and exhibitions of painting and sculpture. Some, no doubt, even read poetry with relish.

At this point it might be insisted that scientific men hold no such antagonistic attitude toward the alleged values of the arts. But if they do not, they should, unless the orthodox scientific attitude is a sort of intellectual business suit not to be worn on special occasions.

Now if we should ask the butcher why he likes music, he would probably find himself at a loss to give an answer that would seem sufficient either to himself or to us. But if we should ask: "Does it somehow seem to lift you out of yourself?" he would agree that it does seem to do that. Pursuing our inquiry among the enthusiastic devotees of the three other arts under consideration, we find them all agreed upon this point; we find that at the moment when one experiences the power of any art at its maximum, there is a sense of exaltation, of expanded awareness, and the loss of one's habitual self. In its most intense form, the experience may be likened, in the words of our Brahmin friend, to the merging of a raindrop with the sea—losing its own limiting sphericity, but gaining the vaster identity of all water. The intensity of the experience will vary, of course, with the power of the artistic stimulus and the sensitiveness of the psychic equipment upon which it acts, so that some who sincerely care for the arts may never experience more than a pleasing sensation from even the greatest work of art; but always the tendency will be found to be in the direction indicated—toward the loss of self in a larger identity. And there will come in the higher reaches of that mood an ecstatic sense of freedom in a larger understanding, however brief; and this will be strangely colored with the sadness of what we call beauty—that backward pull toward the familiar and the dear.

We have undertaken to arrange four arts in a sort of common-sense order of merit, beginning with sculpture, which seemed unquestionably real and therefore rightfully first. Painting, being two-thirds real, was given second place. By a close margin, poetry managed to remain one-third real, and therefore came next. But music, obviously the least real of all, and therefore at the bottom of the scale, easily leaped to first place in its actual appeal to men. From the standpoint of appealing power, we are compelled to reverse our scale, for a little thought should suffice to show that more people are deeply moved by music than by poetry; more are deeply moved by poetry than by painting; more are deeply moved by painting than by sculpture. Then shall we say that in passing from sculpture to music we are ascending? As a matter of fact we are going neither up nor down. We are merely moving away. Away from what, and how? This brings us to what we shall call the creative dream.

It will be noted that the choice of such an expression, for use in what appears to be (but is not) a contest with the reality of common sense, seems to involve a damaging admission. This is due to the fact that by far the greater portion of the average waking life of men is spent with reference to a single focus of attention, the so-called normal one, and that we have therefore a standardized conception of the world. Because this conception is habitual and standardized, we assume without thought that our so-called normal conception of the world includes all of the world. What it includes can be no more than our habitual representation of the world in keeping with the habitual fixed focus of attention. Furthermore, those aspects of the world that can be shared in common by masses of men will naturally be of an order appropriate to the

[92]

lower levels of even the so-called normal state—a level considerably higher, in the quantitative sense than that of the brute, but not much higher in the qualitative sense. And it is this level that, in our time, has been regarded more and more as the level really worth cultivating.

No one, after a little thought, will contend that we are aware of all that exists; and anyone will grant that there is more in the world of a man than in the world of an infant. The very idea of education implies the expansion of consciousness to include a larger representation of the world. It is the representation of the world that changes, and not the world. It is possible to be aware of more relations, and to be aware in different ways. But so long as we are men, and not archangels, the validity of any unusual state of awareness must be judged by the possible effect of its alleged values upon the lives of men. And this is a test that Art must be willing to undergo.

But if two given foci of attention vary widely enough, the representations of each will be to the other as a dream, unless the fact of expansive consciousness be understood and an attempt be made to correlate the values thereof. It is in this sense that we shall use the word dream, in our expression; for it is in this sense that authentic artists are to be called dreamers, and in no other.

Perhaps we can best get at the meaning of our expression by returning to our friend, the butcher. We have noted what choice he made between two plaster figures of a girl, the one having been cast from the living body, the other produced by a truly great sculptor. He chose the former, and the latter seemed no more real to him than a dream. The same attitude was maintained in the case of the two painted pictures of a forest. He chose the photographic representation, and the picture by Inness seemed inferior, lacking reality. A similar choice was made between factual history and the epic poetry of Homer. In each case, the artist, whether sculptor, painter or poet, had regarded his subject matter from the viewpoint of an extended field of attention, and had undertaken to present a given portion of the world in the larger aspect. But owing to the nature of each of these three arts, the artist was forced to do this in terms of things as represented in the standardized field of attention which men commonly share. The butcher could readily recognize the images used in each case as pertaining to the world of which he was aware— for instance, the human body, the forms of trees, the acts and speech of men. Being sense-bound, as we may well say, he had never suspected that other aspects of the world than those known to him by sight and touch might be possible. He therefore judged the work of the sculptor, the painter and the poet by the sense-terms that each used and wholly with reference to the conceptions of the standard-ized field of attention—the common-sense, the po-tentially scientific field; whereas an adequate judg-ment could have been rendered only by one capable, in some degree, of the psychic change through which each artist had passed in the process of creat-ing his work of art.

How, then, can we explain the fact that the butcher responded readily to music, since he was incapable of responding to the three other arts? Because the musician, by the very nature of his art, cannot utilize any forms that are readily recog-nizable as belonging to the world conceived in the standardized field of attention. The butcher could not possibly apply his familiar standard of judg-ment, for in music there was nothing of his world upon which to base a comparison; and, accordingly, by the very fact of his attention to the music, his familiar world and himself as a part of it were lost in another field of attention, approximately that of the composer in the period of creation—a state far different from that in which hogs are butchered and hams are cured; and this in no way discredits the hog and ham state, except as it is assumed to be the only valid one.

In the process of appreciating any work of art, the appreciator undergoes a change of consciousness, approximating that which took place in the producing artist. And in its complete form the appreciation of a truly great work of art would necessarily take on the characteristics of a dream— dream being the term whereby two widely differing fields of attention may describe each other.

In the language of Æsthetics the word empathy has been used to describe the state in which one may appreciate beauty. Empathy, it will be noted, is, by implication, contrasted with sympathy, the former signifying *feeling into* the object of regard, the latter signifying *feeling with* the object regarded. In a sympathetic regard for an object, subject and object remain consciously separate; in an empathic regard the observer is lost in the object. However, the term empathy seems to have been used by way of describing merely a change of attitude within the standardized field of attention, and not a profound literal change from one field to another—a change whereby subject and object are merged and an extended world is discoverable—a world of larger relations, this world largely seen, and quite as real as that which our standardized state reveals to us.

Dr. Bullough has used the term "psychical distance" by way of describing the relation of the appreciator of beauty to the object regarded, "distance," in his sense, signifying a certain apparently necessary detachment from the object of beauty. But, according to our view, the "distance" involved is that of the shifted focus, by which beauty is perceived, from the standard focus by which men ordinarily live, the observer being in no way remote from the object, but lost in it. The difference to be emphasized may seem unimportant at first thought, but the difference is as great as that between a belief in the narrow normal field of reality as the only valid one and a belief in a very wide range of the real, to be perceived by the characteristic process of art—a range of reality so wide that we can but be ignorant of its limits.

The creative dream, then, is the process of reconstructing the ordinary representation of the world in keeping with an expanded view of it; a creative fusing of two views of the world, each of which would normally seem to the other like a dream. And that which is added to the narrower standardized conception of the world by this process is poetry. We commonly hear lovers of the arts referring to the poetry in the form and poise of a sculptured figure, or in the handling of light and shadow and color in a painting, or in a passage of music; and this use of the word is justified by its etymology, the word poetry being derived from the verb, Ποιέω, meaning "to bring to pass, to bring about, to create."

It is to be deplored that the word poetic must be used in describing this distinguishing quality of art, for this term also has passed through a bath of the multitude and thereby lost its meaning. To describe any work as "poetic" is certainly no great compliment as the term is generally understood by those who do not care. To prettify, to ornament and distort with make-believe, is to be poetic; and a poetic poet, in the vulgar sense of the term, is an abomination to poets. The term *poietic* has been coined, and it might well be employed by way of restoring the meaning, leaving the term poetic to prettifiers and make-believers. But one should not quarrel with one's tools; and a tool dulled by much and careless handling may be sharpened for one's

[98]

own use. Poetic can mean *poietic* to us; and its meaning will in no way approach that of the word ornamental. Also, its meaning for us will be psychological rather than literary. For us, a versifier may poetize year after year about birds and roses and sunsets and ladies' eyes and tears and moonbeams and brooks and April showers; and so long as he does all this within the limits of the standardized field of attention, we will not call his product poetic, however much he may decorate it with phrases and epithets. But if, in the whole mood of his production, or at any moment therein, it is evident to us that he must have lost his habitual self and his familiar standardized world in a flash of the wider regard, we will apply the term poetic in all reverence, for it is to the outer reaches of the human that reverence is due.

Now up to this point, as I am aware, it has been possible for a very matter-of-fact person, unacquainted with modern psychology, to insist that everything I have had to say about fields of attention, states of consciousness, is concerned with no more than an arbitrary division of one thing into various imaginary parts, a naming of the parts and a more or less adroit juggling with the names in keeping with a theory. Certainly that sort of thing is common nowadays; and when anyone is caught in the act of flashing a roll of paper money, said to be gold certificates, it is proper to inquire if there be any gold of fact to back the paper. We have been talking about expanded states, and have seemed to credit them with powers transcending those of the standardized state in which the "live-wire" and the go-getting moneyac thrive. Since the creative dream is said to be concerned with expanded states, it may be well to give a single example of such a state by way of reassuring any very practical person who may have survived yesterday's ordeal. Some years ago I witnessed a surgical operataion. The patient was under an anæsthetic and was evidently unaware of pain. Staring blankly at the ceiling, she talked constantly and strangely, often of things not in my experience; and it may or may not be that what she strove to say in her (to me) vaguer moments was merely the nonsense of delirium. But there were other moments that were not vague; for she commented on the facial expressions of those behind her and not visible to her in any physical sense. She chided me for a smile of involuntary amusement at her weird chatter at a time when I could not have been seen by her. Also it was clear to all of us from her remarks that a person passing behind an opaque object in the room remained in some way clearly apparent to her. Upon regaining normal consciousness she was still unable to find words for what may or may not have been nonsense; but she insisted that she had seemed to float above her body, finding it difficult to maintain her connection with it, and that from that vantage point everything was clearly visible in every direction, regardless of what would, normally, have been obstacles to vision. No one would contend that consciousness was lacking, for the patient was aware; nor would anyone contend that her state was identical with the standardized state in which she ordinarily lived, for she was aware of much that in her usual sense-bound state would have been hidden from her, considering her position on the operating table. Nor can one insist that it was all merely a matter of delirium and so without meaning—which is a common lazy method of discrediting such phenomena; for this expanded state of the patient was valid to the extent that certain findings of that state were tested by the standardized state and found correct —a purely common-sense test. I have given this extreme example because it happened to come under my observation and because a great many similar examples have been well authenticated and recorded. The fact of the anæsthetic in no way damages the example for our purpose, since we wish to show merely that an expanded state, with correspondingly expanded powers, is possible.

An artist, we may say, is one whose habit it is to view the world from the vantage point of states more or less removed from the standardized state of ordinary living, and who has a special technique for representing the wider experience by fusion with the narrower, to the end that his vision may be shared.

To make a crude picture of the idea, we may fancy the great mass of men as living in a valley entirely surrounded by lofty mountains. Being so long forced to act as though there were nothing beyond the mountains, most men have come to believe that nothing is real outside the valley. This is their genuine belief, the one upon which they act. Their religion teaches them that there is a wonderful world beyond the mountains, and that those people who are consistently good in the traditional sense of the valley will die into that wider world. But meanwhile the mountains appear to be impassable, and no one altogether "in his senses" strives to climb them. Indeed it would be considered impious to try, as though one should dare to peep before his time upon the secret doings of divinity. But as far back as valley records reach, and far beyond, no doubt, there have been variations of the valley type. Some of these are not sound sleepers, as practical and thoroughly "successful" valley men should be. We may say, by way of making our picture clearer, that some of these variant types become notorious sleepwalkers, and in ways unknown, perhaps, to themselves, manage to ascend the steeps about the valley while other men are deep in slumber. No one sees them come and no one sees them go, for it is a distinguishing characteristic of valley people to sleep a heavy sleep. And when the somnambulist himself undertakes to tell what he has seen below him under the stars and moon, he himself may not know it from the stuff of dreams. But men listen willingly, for there is a novel, entertaining quality, and something mysteriously more, in what these men may undertake to tell. One of them may have viewed the valley from only a moderate height; but even from that vantage point the aspect of familiar things has changed, and new relations are perceived—relations that throw a strange light upon one's thought about one's neighbor, perhaps. Another may have ascended still farther, and from that high viewpoint other changes in the aspect of familiar things are to be recorded, for there the whole valley is seen at a glance, and things once big, grow little, and many things are merged, and much that once seemed to matter, doesn't matter. And now and then it seems that one may have stood upon a swimming peak and beheld the valley as a tiny pool of shadow in a vast of starlight, as though he had peered a moment upon an outer world—but this we are not yet permitted to believe.

Now each of these finds trouble in the telling of what men call his dream; for language has been developed to meet the need of those who have never left the valley, and there are no words for aspects of the valley from the height. Accordingly, through the ages, these sleepwalkers have developed new languages, new techniques, whereby it may be possible to re-create in the minds of valley men some semblance of the vision of the height; and this cannot be done at all unless something of the original mood of the seeing can somehow be produced. Curious strategic devices are employed —devices fashioned for the ear and eye, since, as Jane Harrison has observed in *Ancient Art and Ritual,* these are the organs of the "distant senses." Some strive with color, some with visual form, and some strive to present the mood of the vision by weaving sounds into enchanting patterns. And some use words in ways unknown to common valley parlance, creating a rythmic flow of pictures in the mind of him who hears; and this way is more suggestion than telling, more singing than speech; and were it all a telling, less would be told.

All this is the technique of the arts; and always the effect of the message thus delivered is to set the general above the particular, to emphasize the larger relations, to merge the heedful self in the whole. And at this point it is important to note how Art blends, by imperceptible degrees, into Ethics; while in the realm of its origin it is obviously one process with essential Religion. Some men, in that regard, are very old-fashioned still— men who cannot associate religion with a particular cosmogony, a particular system of rewards and punishments, and a particular ritual, but rather with a passionate desire to understand larger and larger relations, and, so far as these may be ascertained, to be lost in them. And is not every religious dogma an art form[1] originally intended to function as the medium of this same passionate desire for loss of

---

[1] Jane Harrison: *Ancient Art and Ritual.* Frazer: *The Golden Bough.*

[105]

YORK COLLEGE LIBRARY

self in the great process of which we are a part? The sonnet form may be an excellent vehicle for the expression of poetic vision; but if one should come to insist that poetry is a matter of fourteen lines of a given metric pattern arranged in accordance with a stipulated rhyme scheme, one might lose the poetry altogether and come to hate his neighbor for perversely favoring the quatrain. But the artistically pious, as we may say, will insist only that the form used shall be an adequate medium of the poetry, which is the sole justification of the form.

We must note that the picture of the hemmed-in valley with its many sound sleepers and its few somnambulists is accurate enough to convey the desired impression that the standardized vision of the world is not the only possible one, and that visions of the world from expanded fields of attention may be none the less true visions of the world. But our valley picture is, nevertheless, inadequate in one particular; for it had to be based upon the assumption of a sharp line of division drawn between the artist and the valley dwellers. No such sharp line exists, though once a certain penumbra of difference is passed, the division seems sharp enough. There is a great deal in the findings of modern psychology to show that the consciousness of any man extends well beyond that focus which most men deem the only valid one. It is as though one's field of consciousness were a vast sensitive area, reaching how far no one knows; and over this area, to a greater or less degree, shifts the realizing focus of the self.[1] Even the most matter-of-fact man must have experienced this shifting of the focus; and there must have come to him, as a result, moments of swift insight. But if he gives these moments any thought at all, it is generally only to remark to himself how "queer" they were. But probably very few people are as sense-bound as they seem to others or deem themselves to be; and very many, without any knowledge of the process, must live, to some extent, the life of the artist, action being the only form of expression they know. In our sense, then, there is profound meaning in the saying that Man is the artist animal; and in proportion as he utilizes in the standard animal realm the values to be perceived only by the characteristic process of art is he raised, in the qualitative sense, above the status of the brute. How then may we describe the dogmatic materialist? May we not say that he is one who assumes that the only way

[1] Myers: *Human Personality*.

to solve our human problems is by intensifying the focus of light where it impinges on the standardized area of essentially animal experience? Given a microscope of steadily increasing magnifying power, a man might spend a lifetime in the study of a single square foot of sod in his front yard; and it might seem to the man that the square foot of earth was expanding, so long as he kept his eye glued to the microscope, noting the increasing complexity of phenomena; but he would learn nothing of the round earth. Without discrediting the great value of the man's microscopic discoveries, other men, who, perchance, had done a bit of roving in their day, might reasonably insist upon the co-ordinate values of geography. It is only in detail and not in meaning that this illustration is exaggerated.

Returning to what we have agreed to call the creative dream, we can best get at the mechanism of the process involved by limiting our attention to the literary form called poetry, because it is the one of the four arts chosen that utilizes language. Whatever is true of the process in this form of art will apply in general to the other arts; for the nature of the process involved is identical in all, the technique alone being changed in keeping with the medium employed.

We may assume that all the materials utilized by the poet are found in the standardized world, though one who is familiar with the greatest poetry may sometimes be persuaded to think otherwise. It is best for our purpose to assume that all the original material of poetry is of the common-sense world, since this gives us a much needed contact with extremely practical people; and it will be seen that our case is in no way damaged by the assumption. This material may be almost anything of which the average man in his so-called normal state may be aware.

So long as what we have termed the realizing focus of the poet's self remains fixed, nothing is to be noted by him but the usual factual regard of things familiar. But, suddenly, the light spreads about the object of regard, and in proportion as it spreads areas of hitherto hidden meaning are illumined as in a dream; relations normally concealed are suspected or revealed as in a vision. It is in this swift and ecstatic widening of conscious regard that the substance of the poem is conceived, and the substance of it is concerned with the larger relations that are revealed. It is as though one were walking in a cloudy night with a lantern, the glow of which is turned upon a single tree; and the tree is all that is seen. Suddenly, an inundation of sheet lightning reveals the landscape of which the tree was all the while an integral part. It is a thrilling vision, and how shall it be told to men who, for our purpose, may be conceived as knowing their world only as a lantern may reveal it? We know of course that men do not live wholly by our figurative lantern light. They only persuade themselves to believe that they do; and the effect of this persuasion upon the world is what we see.

As we have noted, it has been shown by experiment that a man's field of consciousness extends beyond that spot to which his attention is normally fixed. Myers called this outer field "the subliminal or ultra-marginal consciousness," and it was his purpose to support by experiment his belief, shared as an "over-belief" by James among many others, that this subliminal may be identical with the surviving ego, the soul. We are not concerned with that conception; not that we reject it, but that we want to justify our poetic values with the least possible strain on the credulity of prejudiced common sense. Von Hartman used the term "the Unconscious," but he was concerned with the construction of a cosmic philosophy and he needed an absolute for his purpose; while we are keeping as close as possible to the familiar coast line of the little island where we must live and work with each other. We know that we are in a rowboat, and that it is for master mariners to sail tall ships by the dim star. What we mean by the outer field is what Myers meant, just short of the point where he reached out into the cosmos for possible spiritual relations that need not concern us

It has been shown that this outer field is fundamental and primitive; that its characteristic processes are concerned, not with words, but with images; not with logic, but with analogies, images being linked together in chains of meaning by virtue of likeness, and the images in the farther reaches of the field tend to be generic. Ellis has dealt with this phase of the problem in his *World of Dreams,* and many other investigators have reached the same conclusion. Furthermore, the sense of time and space, as we have it in waking life, drops away in the further reaches. In a dream, time and space are nothing. Any good student has experienced this in moments of intense concentration. No one can do creative thinking and escape the experience.

The poet then, through some shifting of spontaneous attention, may suddenly conceive a given human experience as regarded from the vantage point of the wider field. His new viewpoint may be only slightly removed from the usual viewpoint of common sense, so that the difference between the two views may seem no more than a restatement in a winsome manner, as in the poetry of James Whitcomb Riley; or the difference may be so great as to demand special development on the part of the recipient of the poet's message, as in much of Shelley's work. In either case the poet will find the literal meanings of words, as given in the dictionary, inadequate for his representation of the new view, since language was developed out of the needs of the waking field, except as the poetic process has touched some of them with meaning that is beyond definition. The new vision cannot be stated merely, for this reason; a sense of it must somehow be induced, and the method will be that which is characteristic of the outer field. Likenesses of both sight and sound will be invoked; the specific, which is transient, will tend to merge in the general and abiding; and the farther the new viewpoint is removed from the habitual one, the more pronounced will this tendency become in the expression of the vision. In poetry like that of Riley, the new viewpoint is so near to the habitual one that the likenesses employed may all be within the everyday experience of the average individual. In the poetry of the major poets, the distance may be so great at times that the likenesses employed must be taken from the widest human experience, that of the race, thus becoming unintelligible to those who have only personal experience upon which to draw for understanding. And race-experience, in this sense, will be far more than historical fact. It will be a matter of great moods that have dominated the minds of men, and such moods in turn can be grasped only through other poetic processes; so that certain portions of a major poet's product may reach back for meaning through a poetic succession the beginning of which is lost in antiquity.

Thus we may say that minor poetry is produced in the edge of the outer field, so near to the standard spot that the sense of time and space is still strong, tending to limit expression to the moment and the place. The ultimate practical values of such poetry will partake of the conventional; and later generations, wrapped up in the conventions of their own times and places, may be little moved by poems that thrilled millions in their time. On the other hand, major poetry is produced in the further reaches of the outer field, so distant from the standard spot that the sense of space and time is weakened, or even lost by fits; the moment and the place grow vague, as remembered in a dream, or vanish as memories of the day in the strangely conscious profundity of sleep. The symbols of expression become generic, the fundamentally human is emphasized, the sense of individuality weakens or dies out, the universal is substituted for the particular; for here the poetic process is taking place in human depths

> That yield no foam to any squall of change.

The ultimate values of such poetry may seem to the unlettered reader little related to his conventional moral code; but the ethical principles involved will be found to be those of which all moral codes are but momentary approximations.

Anyone who truly loves poetry has noted that a great line or passage seems old. Holmes' Autocrat remarked this fact, saying in substance that whenever he wrote a good line it seemed not to be his own. That which, in its origin, was unassociated with time cannot but seem old when the time sense is applied to it. For time is a conventional measure of change, which in turn is a matter of unstable relations; therefore the larger relationing of the poetic process would tend to give an impression of permanence, just as distant hills, seen in their larger relations from a rapidly moving train, seem fixed, while the foreground flows away. It is because human life is vexed with ceaseless change that the relative stabilities of art are precious to us; and those relative stabilities are not illusory, for even in change there are principles that endure, and there is an essential humanness that, at least for our brief planetary life, is constant. We cannot live humanly without an abiding sense of such constancies; and it is by virtue of what we have called the creative dream that these may be vividly realized. Judged by the little relations of strictly common-sense living, we all go down to defeat at the last; for the desire to get something is the pitiful obsession of sense-bound men. It is a characteristic animal obsession. But we never get anything, as the nearest undertaker will testify. We give everything, whether we will or not—and every life, viewed from the standpoint of the narrow world of sense, is a pathetic affair. All the hustle and the hope and the worry and the disappointment and the loss and the suffering—and then what? How can it be justified in terms of the local and the individual and the momentary? What but the vision that is of art can reveal the impersonal victory that is wrought of all these numberless little individual defeats? Yet shrewd men are prone to regard the values of art as impractical in the literal sense. Art, we are told—and even many artists agree—is an imaginative means of escape from reality.

Poetry is a means of communication between the stable and universal background of human personality and the flowing foreground of the individual. The act of creating a poem—or any work of art— is an act of translating; and if pure poetry could be created, it would not be literature; it would be music; just as pure music could be conceived only as enchanted silence. The value of a poem is in proportion to the largeness of the mood that it is capable of creating in the properly sensitive recipient. The major inspiration of the poet is concerned with the conception of that mood and not with details of mechanism in the translation of the mood. This explains why it is possible to give intensive technical study to poetry without experiencing that profound change which it is the function of art to produce. The conception of the poem, even though it be long, may be a matter of seconds or minutes by the clock; but the mutterings of clocks are without significance in those deeps where poetry may be conceived; and just as a sleeper may experience an extended dream adventure in the moment of waking, so may the poet conceive in a flash of the wider regard a poem that only the labor of years can translate in terms of sense. And when this has happened to him, significantly enough, he will feel gloriously safe in the cosmos, and his petty self, with its innumerable hurts and fears and desires, will be lost in an overwhelming sense of love for all things and all men— so long as the revealing moment remains vivid. If this mood could last, he might be what men call a saint; his life would be the only expression of his vision, and few men in any generation would be able to interpret it, for the man would be living wholly with reference to the wider awareness. And he might not live long for obvious reasons. Nearly two thousand years ago there was a supreme artist whose life, lived creatively in accordance with a super-brutal vision, remains a tragic masterpiece of marvelous beauty and power. Even though no such person ever lived, as some contend in the drab, impertinent mood of factuality, nevertheless the supreme work of art remains in the conception of such a person. In either case the values and their source remain the same. It is because the poet is incapable of such a life that he is a poet at all. The grip of sense is strong upon him, and by reason of his characteristic swift shiftings of attention, always with a notable intensity, his frailties may exceed, for practical purposes, those of the solid citizen safe within his walls of sense. Some poets will be less able than others to achieve a livable adjustment, and much will depend upon the place and time in which the poet lives.

But when the revealing moment of the conception has passed, the backward swoop of the sensible fact will be like a sickness for home; and in great art something of this is found to be inseparable from beauty. The mood of the poem may be such as to admit of a brief translation, so brief that it may be completed while the original vision is still vivid; or it may require years. In the latter case there must be frequent returns of the original vision lest the mood of the whole, which is the life of the poem, should be lost; and we may see what Poe meant when he said that there could be no long poem. He was saying that, in his own case, it was now or never with a given mood; and he did not take into account the architectural possibilities of a single creative mood often returning and cumulative. It is thus that a tree is builded by many returns of the summer. In our moment of rapid physical development, syncopated haste and fragmentary vision, the point we are considering is likely to be overlooked. In general, our poetic criticism is prone to miss the larger mood, which is architectural, placing undue emphasis upon minor inspirations concerned with technical detail. That the mood of what we have called the major inspiration—the vitalizing mood of the whole—is the matter of fundamental importance, can be demonstrated by merely naming a few great poems. Say *Hamlet* or *Macbeth* or *Lear* or *Agamemnon* or *Œdipus* to a person rich in poetical understanding, and in each case he will be moved by a quick awareness of something powerful and beautiful in a large and wordless sense. That mood is concerned directly with the fundamental greatness of the poem. Only upon second thought are lines and passages remembered. It was that same mood, far more intensely experienced perhaps, that the poet undertook to share with other men; and when it first gripped him, we may be sure he felt for a moment that he must run and tell the world about it. But telling news of that sort to this world of ours is no simple matter.

Pearsall Smith has a yarn in his *Trivia* that illustrates the difficulty. He tells of a gentleman leaving his club late at night after an evening not lacking in cheer of a pre-Volsteadian character. And as the gentleman rode homeward in the starlight, an overpowering sense of the vastness of the heavens and the wonders of creation came upon him. Suddenly, in a flash of vision, he knew the secret of the universe. He knew that he knew it by the wind of glory that swept him as a harp and hurt him as with song. Illumined with a white flare of love for all men and all things he said: "I must tell the human race of this!" But at the thought of the world, the vision faded, for he knew just what the world would say. Indignant now and deeply hurt, he shouted: "No one has any right to say I am drunk!"

We must admit, with all appropriate symptoms of moral shock, that our homebound clubman was artificially, even illegally, illuminated. Yet we cannot be certain that he had not, for a moment, such news as men might profitably hear. The trouble was that his mood evidently covered far too much territory for his capacity as a translator.

But though the fundamental greatness of a poem is commensurate with the mood of the whole, even as the fundamental greatness of Nebraska's new capitol is in the totality of the architectural dream, yet either, to be of value, must be shared; and the process of sharing, of translating the mood, may be a gruelling task; but, in keeping with the timelessness of the wider field in which such moods can be conceived, no artist of any consequence will balk at time. Being lost in the mood, he will give all his years for it if necessary, even though he may fear, in his moments of lapse, that no one will ever care and that he may be throwing his life away. It is his business to throw himself away; and always, in his deeper moods, he knows this and is thrilled with the knowledge.

Blue prints fix the mood for the architect's build-ers; but the poet is his own builder, and in any extended work he must depend not only upon fre-quent returns of the original vision of the whole, lest the mood he strives to fix be lost, but also upon many minor flashes of a wider regard concerned with the details of the structure—the use of sym-bols and rhythms and sounds in such a way as to produce by cumulative means the mood of the whole which it is his sole purpose to build up in others through the inadequate medium of sense. Then, when the structure is completed, there may be those

well-meaning admirers who will attempt to show
their appreciation solely by pointing out felicitous
epithets, striking lines, impressive passages. And
these, indeed, are of great importance; but,
after all, they exist only for the mood of the
whole, and are secondary. An ugly building could be
constructed of the finest marble exquisitely carven;
a supremely beautiful building could be made wholly
of steel and concrete. This is not equivalent to
saying that a supremely beautiful building cannot
be made of marble exquisitely carven; yet in poetry,
as in the other arts, a forthright bareness in the
detail may sometimes serve to intensify the mood
of the whole; and, on the other hand, excessive richness in detail may easily blur the mood. Yet it is
detail that is most commonly noted in our time of
much analysis and little synthesis.

Gordon Bottomley has a remarkable poem on
The Last of Helen that is like a collection of pearls
and rubies and sapphires and diamonds. Strange
fires flash from costly words in a truly wonderful
manner. There are many brief consecutive enchant-
ments, but not a cumulative one; and even the ad-
miring reader ends in bewilderment. It is like
beautiful chords and arpeggios lacking a single cre-

ative mood to bind them into a magical unity. Walter de la Mare's lyric, *The Listeners*, serves to show how powerful a single mood can be builded without any richness of detail, but solely by keeping the mood and making pictures and sounds and even the uneasy movement of the lines contribute cumulatively to the production of an overpowering sense of regret and heartache and loneliness.

> "Is there anybody there?" said the Traveller,
> Knocking at the moonlit door;
> And his horse in the silence champed the grasses
> Of the forest's ferny floor:
> And a bird flew up out of the turret
> Above the Traveller's head:
> And he smote upon the door a second time;
> "Is there anybody there?" he said.

In detail this poem is scarcely poetic at all, as the word is popularly used; but it is intensely *poietic* in the original constructive sense—the only sense in which any work of art can achieve greatness. It is true that a great creative personality will show greatness in the quality of his minor inspirations of detail, though not necessarily with the result of quotability; but if one were forced to choose—and happily there is no such choice demanded—between a profound sense of the great human mood that is the *Iliad* on the one hand, and an appreciative memory of separate Homeric epithets, lines, passages, on the other, it is the latter that should be sacrificed, for the supreme social value is in the former—a value that is ethical in the broadest practical sense.

The appreciation of the point we have been noting is apparent to anyone who has been called upon to read much verse produced by the average tyro. Almost always, in such cases, it is the technical detail of poetry that is imitated. The effort, as we may say in popular phrasing, is to make a noise like poetry; and one might be considered over-harsh if, in criticising such an effort, he should remark that the verses needed to be rewritten on a different theme by some other poet. Yet the criticism would more often be right than wrong, since the poetic mood of the whole, which is the major product of the creative dream, is the matter of fundamental importance in any art. The fatal fact about our average tyro is that he has not for a moment conceived his material outside the standardized field of sense, and he is imitating that special aspect of poetry which is concerned necessarily with the standardized field. He simply has nothing to convey that is not of the standard field commonly shared by all men.

Assuming, in any case, an authentic mood to be conveyed—a mood originating in the wider regard of the outer field with its correspondingly extended awareness of relations—poets may differ greatly in the character of that about which the mood is cast, in their methods of translation, and in the degree of success attained therein. In Blake, for instance, we have a striking example of inability to represent the outer view in terms of the standard view, the latter seeming to have been by far the vaguer to Blake. His drawings reveal the same inability to fuse the two views; and it is for this reason that he is an artist for artists, a "poet's poet." But after all differences are noted, there will remain a fundamental likeness, which will relate all authentic poets in a long line disappearing in the further glooms of history. Capable criticism, of which there has never been much, must be concerned, first of all, with the identification of that something which relates the latest authentic poet with the earliest. You will remember how Æschylus describes the sending of the signal from fallen Ilion to waiting Argos—hill and peak and crag and isle and jutting headland flashing sequent beards of fire that the news of victory might be known to men. The poets are like that, though now a tall fir flames golden like the sun and now a heap of gray old heather flings a smokier glow. And what is this news of victory, in our sense, but the news of those wider relations, an abiding awareness of which alone can make life other than the outrageous indignity it must seem, and is, when confined to what so many in our day conceive to be its necessary limits?

This fundamental likeness which relates all poets —and all artists are poets—is not in itself a matter of descent, of tradition handed down from bard to bard across the gaps of changing tongues and times. It is true that they give and borrow both mood and technique, all along the line, so that there is truth enough in Hugo's saying that the poets are "a long line of gentlemen with their hands in each other's pockets." It is because of this fact that there is a powerful cumulative effect in the reading of World Literature that no person of narrow literary experience can hope to comprehend. But the fundamental likeness that relates them is due to the practical identity of the deeper and relatively stable states from which, at their representative best, they all view the flowing world. This likeness, when genuine, is spontaneous and independent in the personality of every new poet as he rises.[1] It is in the matter of translating that there is traditional descent.

Not only is poetry autogeneous in every poet; it is also inevitable in the very nature of expansive human consciousness, though certain times and societies will favor its emergence in art while others will determine other creative outlets for the faculty.

> Had Milton called on Jaweh, so to speak,
> About the middle of His busy week;
> Beheld the plastic hands with chaos smeared,
> The viscid muck of planets in His beard
> And all those mud balls waiting to be twirled—
> Could Milton then have sung the pendent world
> Close by the moon? And neither could he sing
> Of pious regicide and headless king,
> But gave to arid sesquipedal prose
> The billingsgate of his Defensios—
> Thunder gone mousing!

[1] "Kill off every known and suspected poet, and there will be as many as ever after a generation or two. If the language were destroyed, ages would be needed to evolve another; but poetry, being a constant function of life, is rooted as it were perpendicularly in every moment of consciousness, and not horizontally, trailing back long feelers into mist-hidden swamps of primitiveness."— John Erskine: *The Kinds of Poetry.*

Lo, ten thousand Greeks
Marched up the East with Cyrus; scaled the peaks
Of epic venture; yet not one returned
With half a distich!   They were more concerned
With keeping whole while carving up their neighbors,
The union scale of wages for their labors,
And longing for the unsymbolic sea,
Than with the trope-craft of Calliope!

And if, to cheat the prying scholiast,
Old Homer lived, 'tis certain that he cast
No biting bronze along Scamander stream.
Incantatory trumpets of a dream
Called from the hinter gloom, and he beheld
Troy towers tottering in a flare of Eld,
With Helen's face a storm-moon through the smoke.

When men are constrained to act, they do so
creatively in their degree and manner.   And it is
worth noting in this connection that in supreme
moments of action this characteristic process, which
is art's, is certain to occur, though it is not generally recognized as such.   Forsyth's fifty scouts
fought as in the exaltation of a timeless dream at
the moment when eight hundred mounted warriors
under Roman Nose charged howling down in solid
mass upon their little sandy island in the Rickaree.
This is simply to say that they fought with the

whole range of the man; and when this happens, the self is lost and unsuspected human powers are released for use. In *The Gambler* Dostoevsky describes this characteristic state as experienced by a heavy winner at roulette. It is the gambler who speaks: "Black won. I don't remember my winnings after, nor what I staked on. I only remember, as though in a dream, that I won. I only remember that I gathered up money in thousands. At times a glimmer of prudence (this is the standard state) dawned upon me. I would cling to certain numbers and combinations, but soon abandoned them and staked almost unconsciously. I must have been very absent-minded. . . . Suddenly there were sounds of loud talk and laughter and everyone cried 'Bravo!' Some even clapped their hands." The bank, unable to pay further losses, had closed for the night.

We say that the gambler had "a run of luck," and the point need not be argued; yet it is not to be doubted by anyone who has had certain experiences, bearing the test of comparison with objective fact, that in ways not under control the outer field may be literally aware of much that is commonly hidden. I myself know of a case in which a poet described a vast country in topographical detail and with photographic accuracy, although he had never seen the country and had no recognized means of knowing it.

We have noted such lower manifestations of the creative dream in order to emphasize the fact that it is inevitable in human consciousness, whether the result be act or art; and only by identifying it throughout the activities of men can we see that it is humanly inevitable. It would seem that the important thing is to educate and guide that power for social uses.

If this fact were better understood by critics, we should not be hearing, as every generation is forced to hear, the dreary old assertion that poetry is of the past and that men are now too wisely practical to produce great poets. Before the great war one heard the same sort of thing about heroism, an allied phenomenon. But there were some who, knowing men, knew better. Prof. F. C. Prescott, in his generally admirable and illuminating study of *The Poetic Mind,* falls into the old dreary error. He says: "The real difficulty is that, as we no longer have the imagination to write poetry, we lack even the imagination to read it. The age of poetry is gone; that of sophisters, scholiasts, and antiquarians has succeeded. We must spend our time threshing over the remains of former harvests." Now poetry has always been dead according to the Prescotts of the moment, who could recognize neither Shelley nor Keats, to name only two of many; but if any widely known iconoclast should be so bold as to contend now that Shelley and Keats were not great poets, every Prescott of our time could prove the opposite with an imposing display of erudition. They would be right, but not by virtue of any ability to judge poetry independently, since they would be quite as ready to prove the next great poet of little if any consequence, and with the same imposing display of erudition. They simply do not know, as the history of criticism proves; and there are things written by the greatest of the old poets that are so poor that no respectable magazine would print them as fillers if they were written now; yet some of these things have been held up as beyond the power of any modern poet to equal. The difficulty lies in the fact that past poetical greatness is reduced to a formula in keeping with the translational structure, whereas it is precisely in the translation of the poetic mood that poets may differ most. Effective criticism must be concerned, first of all, with the recognition of that in all poets which is fundamentally identical. Criticism is not and cannot be a matter of factual knowledge, of formula; it is altogether a matter of the development of the poetic consciousness in the critic. The judgment must be within the mood of the poem considered, and no amount of judging from the outside will be of the slightest use. Criticism of poetry in this fundamental and necessary sense cannot be taught. One might as well attempt to study saintliness from its manifestations by way of becoming a saint. It is a matter of profound change within the personality, and there are no rules whereby such a change can be achieved, just as there are no rules whereby saintliness or heroism can be achieved.

Prof. Prescott's error in the passage quoted is due to this: that he based his judgment upon a theory formulated independently of the facts. He begins with the curious assumption that genuine poetry is not being written now, and if he were not himself a thresher of former harvests, he could have known better. It would be easy to name many authentic poets, now living, who are not to be annihilated by the blindness of scholars—always one of the tremendous forces of the world. The assumption, at variance with the fact, is to be supported as follows, if at all: Men have become scientific in their attitudes. Science is matter-of-fact, whereas poetry is of the imagination. Men with the scientific outlook cannot be poets or even love poetry.

But without imagination modern science would have been impossible. So obvious is this that in its higher reaches it approximates the poetical. Furthermore, when and for what reason did the outer field of human consciousness, itself a fact of science, suddenly become inoperative in men? We are only now beginning to learn something about that outer field, and further knowledge of it is certain to revolutionize our thinking and our attitudes. If poetry can no longer be written or even read with understanding, why waste one's time in writing a book about it? Happily, it is the great merit of Prof. Prescott's discussion—which is based wholly upon the fact of an outer field of consciousness—to disprove in numerous ways the unfortunate statement noted.

Neither science nor poetry could dispense with imagination. But we lose our way with Prof. Prescott if we accept the ordinary meaning of the term, as being concerned, necessarily, with unreality. We must think of imagination, in this connection, as a wider revelation of reality through a supersensible awareness of larger relations, the process being concerned with the linking of images in keeping with the wordless character of the wider field.

The error in criticism of poetry here emphasized is far more than a matter of erroneous opinion in the field of art. It is a social error with profound ethical consequences in the everyday life of men. We must come to realize the significance of the fact that there is a wide range of valid states of consciousness; that expanded consciousness, out of which genuine art grows, is not a matter of imagination in the ordinary sense of unreality, but of imagination in the literal sense of representing by images an extended view of reality by which alone it is possible to live humanly. The world can be no more for us than that representation of it which is built up in us, and the dogmatic common-sense man therefore limits his world to the one standardized spot upon which his attention is rigidly fixed. But the whole of a man must be the whole of his conscious field and his world is limited in reality to what his consciousness can realize. We are generally far less than half men in our normal relations, we may be sure, and our materialistic society exists in a very small fraction of the humanly realizable world.

The technique of art is the technique of an extended attention, realizing an extended world through its larger relations. The values of art are, for that reason, fundamental ethical values in the broadest practical sense, without which there can be no genuine education; and any society, however complex, will be civilized in proportion as it admits these values as real and integral in its scheme of practical things. To regard the arts as merely entertaining, or as a means of escape from reality, is to miss the point utterly and to lose the values. These values are called humanistic, and for a good reason, as we see; but if we should give the name animalistic to the values of materialistic science, we might make our meaning clearer for those who must have all their ideas neatly boxed off from each other; but all values must be interdependent, as the parts of any whole are interdependent. To ignore the higher is to have no human justification for the lower; and to deny the lower is to have nothing upon which the higher may act.

Since the narrow standard field is that for which speech evolves and manners and customs develop, it is only in this field that men may differ hopelessly. Modern psychology shows that, as the outer field is penetrated, differences drop away; and since it is the purpose of art to represent the wider world, art tends to become, as has often been said, but generally with no convincing reason for the saying, the one universal means of communion, not only between individuals of the same race, who are so often separated in a pitiful fashion, but between different races and times. Science, in so far as it insists exclusively upon the reality of the narrower field, can differentiate; the art consciousness alone can identify men. The process of identification is the creative dream, the loss of self in a wider regard of the object.

It will have been seen by this time that my purpose is in no way concerned with "Art for Art's sake." Though I have spent all my years since boyhood on the art of poetry—and at a cost that was sometimes hard to pay—I have not fallen into the belief that even the greatest poetry is important in itself. Life itself is everything, and both art and science are merely strategic methods by which men may live more fully. If art is not concerned with the actual revelation of a wider world, then let men seek momentary forgetfulness by cheaper means. It would be better still, if the prevailing notion of human life and relations were true, to concentrate our energies on the production of lethal gas to be released all over the world at a given moment—a last tremendous act of courage, fit to thrill with admiration the least gentlemanly god that men have ever wrought out of their own fears and cruelties to each other. But there is no justification for despair. Young as we are on this planet, and terrible as has been our experience, we have succeeded in evolving super-brutal values that can save us whenever they shall come into practical use; and those values grow out of the wider visioning that results in art.

If art be an actual continuous revelation of a wider and more humanly habitable world, then what can we expect of a society that is controlled by shrewd, "practical," sense-bound men who base their schemes upon the conceptions and petty personalisms of the narrow field of brutal values? There was certainly meaning in the saying that without vision the people perish; but we have an ingenious way of killing the vital meaning of such sayings by sentimentalizing them in order that we need not act upon them.

What then, from our viewpoint, shall we hope for men—that they all become artists? Waiving the absurdity, we must agree with the Philistine that in a world composed exclusively of artists in the strict sense it would be a long, lean way to a square meal. It is so for millions now, despite the fruitfulness of the earth and the brilliant triumphs of science. Either extreme is humanly impossible. There are some who profess to believe that mankind is slowly evolving cosmic consciousness, and Dr. Bucke,[1] who has presented this hope, foresees the remote time when all men will be geniuses by virtue of this alleged evolution of consciousness toward a comprehensive sense of the whole. But it is a pitiful human trait to place happiness miraculously in the dim future; and our problem is concerned with living here now as men, not a million years hence or some place else as archangels. How may we best do this in keeping with our necessary limitations? Can it be done otherwise than through a new social persuasion determining a system of education designed to introduce all men, in so far as the capacity exists in each, into the realm of those values we have been considering? Such a scheme of education would certainly result in the development of a wider field of consciousness, by which alone it is possible to be human, to identify oneself with the race, and to be moved to throw oneself away in the furthering of as much of the great process as one can perceive.

[1] R. M. Bucke: *Cosmic Consciousness.*

This phase of a more humane education would be concerned less with facts to be learned than with a profound change in one's habitual view of the world and one's relation to it. Such changes are from within, and no amount of preaching can ever produce them from without. They are not effected by the most expert administering of information, but by habitual association with the wider field of regard in which they must occur.

Such an education, in which human values would actually be placed above brutal values, could not produce a world of geniuses, such as Bucke has dreamed; but if we accept, as I think we must, Myers' definition of genius as being concerned with a controlled interplay of the powers of the wider and narrower fields of consciousness, such an education could be expected to approximate *a genius world,* which is a very different idea—that is to say, a world in which the sense-bound mass would be shepherded by men of the wider awareness. The fact that a recognizable approximation of such a genius society once existed briefly in ancient Athens, and with results that still linger as a great light for those who can see it, should give some substance to the hope that has been expressed. The supreme achievement of that approximation of a genius society may be summed up in the one word, σωφροσύνη—a word for which, significantly enough, we have no adequate synonym, since we have in our lives no corresponding synthetic view of the whole range of inter-related human values. We express in English the meaning of that one Greek term by overlaying word with word—a characteristic necessity, due to our broken, fragmentary conception of Man.

The world has not always been insanely desirous of material things and will not always be so. The evolution of materialistic science is bound in a hopeful direction; and anyone who has been awake to the powerful trends of the world, must have felt how the authoritative walls of sense, built up about us by Victorian science, have seemed to be growing thinner of late. There is a widespread yearning for the "more" of which James spoke; and scientific heresy in the realm of psychical research is a healthy sign, whatever may come of it.

In discussing the outer field and its employment in the art process for the production of indispensable human values, I have kept within the limitations set by accredited psychologists. I have referred to the outer field as though it were merely an extension of normal consciousness, revealing more of our common world through an apprehension of relations normally hidden. But many of our best minds all over the world are convinced that what we have called the outer field is in fact the surviving personality—the soul. This conviction, whether justified or not, has been reached through experiment. I would not emphasize this view, for without it there is support enough for the position taken. *But what if it should prove to be true?*

In the meanwhile our schools are designed to produce fractional men by the million, and the emphasis of life is placed on the extreme lower range of humanly realizable values. We are trying to live by bread alone, with far less than half of reality; and through the jungles of the world stalk monstrous hates and greeds, and even in the press of thousands upon thousands of our fellow creatures we are lonesome. With the prevailing conception of Man, how can we hope to live humanly together? Our very understanding is in a state of anarchy, since we are trying to appraise everything by the standards of the one state in which materialism and individualism are possible? The individualistic attitude is well fitted to develop the analytical faculty, but a comprehensive synthesis is beyond it, and truth is in synthesis. The analytical tendency of our time has resulted in a vast accumulation of facts that are to the livable truth as broken pieces of glass are to a window pane. What knowledge we have of the various aspects of a human being are pigeonholed and kept apart, so that we can have no really adequate conception of a man. To the economist he is one thing; to the biologist, he is something else; to the religionist, something utterly unlike what the biologist sees; to the psychologist again he is different; and to the artist he is, in a sense, all that the others see, and yet not at all what is seen by the others. Even our anti-individualistic social reformers, having conceived the social view, would usher in the millennium by shifting relations solely within the economic realm, ignoring the larger man. They themselves are under the hypnotic influence of the very conception of life to which they deem themselves opposed, not suspecting, what we have been emphasizing, that the social view must be concerned with all human values properly related; that the whole realizable range of the human being must be synthetically conceived, and that it is only from such a conception of the entire man, well established in the minds of men, that a human social scheme can be projected upon the world.

We have not been greatly changed by all the

formal creeds of all the centuries of dogmatic strife; for a creed runs readily on the lips and may signify no change in the consciousness of him who repeats it. Only by the general widening of the conscious field in which men act can we hope to live down our animal ancestry and set up standards of value that are human. Only by the systematic stimulation of the art consciousness in men and its application to the problems of society can we hope to be saved from ourselves. We have within us the means of our salvation. So may we yet hope to see for each other, each in his own manner and degree, that shining Camelot of which Tennyson's old seer chanted to young Gareth craving high adventure:

> "For truly, as thou sayest, a Fairy King
> And Fairy Queens have built the city, son; . . .
> And as thou sayest, it is enchanted, son,
> For there is nothing in it as it seems,
> Saving the King; though some there be that hold
> The King a shadow and the city real;
> Yet take thou heed of him, for so thou pass
> Beneath this archway, then wilt thou become
> A thrall to his enchantments, for the King
> Will bind thee by such vows as is a shame
> A man should not be bound by, yet the which
> No man can keep; but so thou dread to swear,
> Pass not beneath the gateway, but abide

Without among the cattle of the field.
For, an ye heard a music, like enow
They are building still, seeing the city is built
To music, therefore never built at all,
And therefore built forever."

YORK COLLEGE LIBRARY

YORK COLLEGE

Library No. ~~44495~~

25659